Daughterbody I

ALSO BY LAURA GENTILE

Within Paravent Walls (a novel)

Daughterbody I
a self-exorcism through poetry

Laura Gentile

DAUGHTERBODY I
Copyright © 2021 by Laura Gentile
Instagram: croque_melpomene

No part of this book may be used or reproduced
in any manner whatsoever without written permission
by the author except in the case of reprints
in the form of reviews

All rights reserved

ISBN 9798538660971

Book design by LAURA KINCAID
Website: tenthousand.co.uk
Instagram: tenthousandlk

Cover art by MAYA BECK
"WHERE ARE U"
Website: mayavanbeek.com
Instagram: mayavanbeek_art

Author photo by PERRY JONSSON
Website: perryjonssonart.com

Printed by Amazon

To Luise, Gisela & Heike

My poems stem from my ancestral bodies to my own.

They have been in the making through generations.

The transgenerational trauma of the past finds transgenerational healing in the present.

I am not alone when I write.

Body of Poetry

Action Figure	1
Unreliability	4
Daddy Deceit Silhouette	6
What You Were Willing To Do	8
Gourmandise | *Daddy Insatiable* | Daughtermemory	9
Daughterobject | Absencepoison | Presencekiller	11
Something's Wrong	12
Mad Girl Straight Into All Of Your Faces	13
Tochterbrustbild | Gunshotlove | A Poem Around Your Edges	15
The Child Can Speak | A Poem, On Two Feet	17
Fatherfiguregirls | A Midnight Poem	20
That's Not How You Say My Name | Out Of Your Mouth | A Poem | Thievery In The Name Of The Father	23
Hands Off | Mind Off | Turn Off	26
Fatherjaw | Daughterfist	28
Fathertongue | Daughtererasure	30
Transferral Of Trauma | In Good Faith	32
Anticipation / Deterioration	34
Nothing Made You Feel Better Than Girls Betraying Each Other For Your Attention	36
Deprivation / Embrace / Toxicity | From Your Body Into Every Letter	39
The Truth In Your Lies | Fatherdaughterface	41
Womansilhouette / Fathertantrum / Wardrumchemistry	43
Girlspine / Daughterendurance / *Father Maniacal*	45
Heartland / Whispers White	47
Ashwaterdaughter / Daughterhair | Self-exorcism	49

Girlmouth / Fathertwig / Daughterporcelain	51
Daughtermouth | Daddyruins	53
Daughtertongue | Swallow	56
Aren't You Full Yet? | All I Could Think About	58
The Apple Came With Maggots All Along	60
Eruption / Destruction / Evocation / Recreation | A Poem Despite All Of Your Efforts	62
Dragging In An Audience | Taking Part In Your Mental Illness	65
In Rejection Of Your Saints | Tell Them Yourself	67
Keeping Your Gargoyles At Bay | You Told Me To Be Silent | Walking Through Marshlands	69
A Phantom On Its Knees	71
Down Your Throat My Language Goes | Rub Your Face In It	73
Drained / Exit Wound	76
Poison Ivy & Ghosts Sitting On Rooftops	78
All The Words You Left Behind	80
A Body Within A Body Within A Body	83
Dirty Fingernails	85
You Tried To Take My Own Language Away From Me	86
The Archaeologist's Memory	88
When The Girl Stopped Pleading	89
The Birth Of Venus	91
The Ingestion Of Terror	93
The Light In My Bones	95
Will You Make Yourself Sick?	97
The Language Of Memorabilia	99
The Butcher Of Intuition	101
Dialogues Passing By	102
Autumnal Introspections | Inner Child	104
Nuances	105
From A To Z And Nothing In-between	106
Rope & Leash	108
Force-fed	110
To Know What Rings True	111
Moths Amidst Fireworks	114

Burn The House Down	115
Pantomime	116
Daughterprey	117
Genii locorum	119
Mea culpā, mea culpā, mea máxima culpa	121
The Spectacle Of Disintegration	123
Die unersättliche Gier der Drangsale: Tribulations Of Insatiable Greed	125
Daughterperspective	127
Healing Just One Part At Least	128
Totenstille / Deathly Quiet	130
Auseinandersetzung / Altercation	131
Internalising The Body Language Of Ghosts	133
Urteilsvermögen / Discernment	136
Using A Little Girl As A Pawn To Win A Game That Is None	139
Ausgangspunkt / Point Of Origin	141
Häufchen Elend / Picture Of Misery	144
The Projectionist	147
Vergissmeinnicht / Forget-me-not	149
Herzkrampf / Heart Spasm	150
Selbstkasteiung / Self-mortification	151
Forging Memories	153
Beschwörung / Evocation	156
Unausstehlich / Insufferable	157
Schamlos / Shameless	159
Widerwärtig / Sickening	161
Bonhomme	164
Basementgirl | Monsterstory	166
În nōmine Pătris	168

Action Figure

I pretended to not be me
I made myself believe
that I was who they asked me to be
the role that made them like me
the part that put a smile on adults' faces
the face that took you in
despite the gut screaming *no*
*
you made me
not listen to my own body
*
I
un-learned
the word
no
from you
*
women were
not supposed
to say *no*
to you
*
you internalised *yes*
to such a degree
that a *no* sounded
unbelievable
*

you taught me
that what I say
doesn't mean anything
it
can
only
get
me
killed
*
I am sick of their faces
the disintegration
the degeneration
I am growing old against them
*
I unbury the past
so that I can name the graves
*
if only I would stand as firmly behind
all the actions of my past
as I stand behind my poetry
*
you don't deserve the big picture
*
nobody knows my mistakes better than I do
and I decide what makes them mistakes
*
do you think that I need your conscience instead of mine?
*
where do we stand now
you and I
*
I don't know how to approach
a liar who believes in his own lies
*

and thinks I'm insane
for taking a step back
*

in your head
there's only one perspective
and it has never been more than that
and yet you invite me over
and lock the door
*

you thought you were so smart
acting like my father

Unreliability

I am not blaming you for the world that I live in
I am blaming you
for the part you played
in mine
when you shrank it
and when you took complete control
without responsibility
when I depended on you
when I was too young
to not cling to you
to escape
to see through you
and understand that I am safe(r) on my own
*
oh
you
spat
fire
and
I
swallowed
it
all
*
every time
that I tried
to get close to you

I looked at your face
and felt
an abyss open up
between us
*
and you'd let me fall
*
I'd never come closer
*
silence
floating above the abyss
no warnings
no cautionary tale
if you come closer you'll die
*
but you didn't keep your hands to yourself

Daddy Deceit Silhouette

when you
incessantly told me
to stop eating,
what image did you have in mind?
*
and I learned
that you and I
had a similar face
carved out of the same material
I want my lines to have a different meaning
I want my face to be able to feel release
I want the truth on my face
not the lies that rubbed off
*
you taught me to believe in canons
in people doing it better
accumulating the world
closing their doors
the golden institutions
to seek their approval
at the cost of everything
at the cost of un-becoming myself
and that was a small price to pay
in your eyes
*
who could I
your daughter

ever become
anyways
making all the wrong choices
*
you
would
never
tell
me
the
truth
and
now
you
beg
for
my
love

What You Were Willing To Do

You rattled something within me
That should have woken up on its own,
In its own time, on my accord, but you wouldn't wait,
You couldn't wait, you wanted control,
You wanted to inject yourself, intercept, determine.
You needed everything from me.

Since my birth, you were thirsty and hungry.

You always came first, I never entered your picture at all.
You pretended as if we didn't exist, existed too much,
As if we didn't belong to you,
Out of your control and influence, creatures apart,
Speechless, languageless, useless, an embarrassment,
Failures, nobody ever seemed to wonder, to question you,
Your lack of actions and dialogue,
And the overdose of thoughtless cruelty that got stuck in
  my brain.

So many times you drove us purposefully into our near
  deaths,
You, the man who conjured up his own in his mouth
During his entire life as if it were all a grand old rotten show,
No, you would never go down all alone, you drag people
  with you,
Your own flesh and blood down with you,
I can't believe that I still got into a car with you.

Gourmandise | *Daddy Insatiable* | Daughtermemory

Keeping you company
Was more important
Than my own life,
That's what you taught me.

It doesn't matter if I die
As long as I'm here for you.

It doesn't matter if I live
If I don't stand by you.

The only organic stir
In relation to you
Was self-preserving violence.

I wanted to live
And you were so ashamed
By what you brought
Into this world.

Looking at yourself in mirrors,
You rejected your own fatherhood.

You had no responsibilities,
You made *all these sacrifices*
That I could never find, that were never my fault,
You created us so that you could free yourself from your

demons that baptised us,
And it backfired, you couldn't stand it, us, your face in ours
    gazing back at you,
And your self-loathing infected our bodies.

You never taught us your language and
Wondered why we lived in a different world.
As we grew up you beat us down.

That was your language.

My father's body language.

The rot coming out of the mouth.

Against women (you still smelled of them).

Against your children (I am not your possession).

My father fucks and fucks and plays the grand seducer,
And I see women fall and fall into despair and turn into
    sad little girls,
He was a seeker and he found what he was looking for,
A bargain hunter with a killer instinct, slow and profound,
First the mind, then the body.

I see women shrink and metamorphose into caricatures
That he mocks and sucks on and moulds into bones with
    his spit
And he shines and gives himself applause
Because he eats us all alive and we feel oh so precious on
    that silver platter.

Daughterobject | Absencepoison | Presencekiller

We lay in the consequences of your actions,
Blood red, tired to the bone, I sank out of myself,
Leaking, I stopped wishing to become an adult,
I just looked at the floor that held pieces of me
And smelled my tears dry, your body behind mine,

Are you done now, are you done now?

I thought you'd never end.

There was no time, no space, I stopped moving amongst
 the shards.
You accepted me like this, broken down, collecting bits
That you wanted, apart from my whole body.
Suddenly you felt alive again and I stopped speaking.
I had enough of you.

You imitated love, you mimicked affection, you terrified
 me,
Looking into me as if we shared a secret or too many,
As if I could remember, your poignant smile, the forbidden
 appetite,
Who are you? Who were you? Your eyes on me always felt
 insane.
I projected lovability onto your face in order to soothe my
 inherited fear.

Something's Wrong

You led multiple lives when you created me.
Scarred me before I had skin and bone.
There will be no more teachers at my mother's door.

I write what I want, they can't take it, he pretends,
Holding on to his fake laurels, his distorted memory,
I reject your sickness, the world enrages me.

I ignited revolutions as a child until they told me one
Too many times to kneel and crouch and bite my tongue.
Daddy likes women on their knees.

He calls them names, but he wants them, wants them,
Restaurants, basements, Daddy lives in many different worlds.
A man of culture, of eloquence and grand gestures he fools them all
And rises higher and higher and yet runs around in circles,
In *repetitions*, women beg him with their mouths open
Because they believe him, but he devours them,
Sucks them dry, feeds his little boy soul, *Maestro*, as if in search of his mother's nipple,
This grown man who throws children out of windows,
This grotesque *father figure theatrical* absorbs women's lives
To kill his soul and erect his ego.

Mad Girl Straight
Into All Of Your Faces

There are cruel subtle sentences outside of my body
Telling me that I do not exist.
They take my body for granted, my tired and composed
　　smile reaching out of an abyss.
I'd put it all out in the open if they'd let me, if I could
And I can indeed, burst, and scream it out into the world
Of people asking how I am and not waiting for the answer,
Not wanting to hear the truth, the tritone of lies, good,
　　good, good,
As in bla bla bla, and the fires within me spread wider and
　　harder.

There are sentences of my ancestors in women's bodies,
From one to another, split, in circles, in agony and worship,
We crave to bond, to hold onto each other without letting
The inside men break us, tell us lies, their stench and filth,
Crude silver, copper coins, dirt, into the dust with you all,
The past and the present are a braid that I won't cut off,
You'll see I jump around a lot from one moment to next,
See, how we are all connected still and always have been?
My childhood affects my womanhood, dig into the mess
　　in-between.
Past behavioural patterns seek their symmetry in the
　　present.
I was part of my mother's body to say the least.
I lived within her.

I am my grandfather's granddaughter. I am my father's daughter.
When you created me you wanted to profit, get it all out and in.
The careless gesture, a ghost, irresponsibility, thoughtless,
Animalistic, getting rid of, exorcised, disembodied.
That's him, hunting for what makes him feel good for a heartbeat instant.

A body language that makes her gag, makes her want to forget,
That she shoves into the depths of her body,
The garbage mouth in the back of her head, taking him in.

And he pretends to be proud, then insults me, then licks his lips,
His friends, too. Men of neglect, men of abandonment derail me
In their absence, scar me with their presence, I kept my eyes open,
Lights out, pillow on the face, eye to eye, putting my cards on the table,
They shoved a silver tongue into my throat and I forged it into a sword.

Tochterbrustbild | Gunshotlove | A Poem Around Your Edges

When you put the word *love* in your mouth,
All I feel is rage.

When you tried to touch me in an affectionate way,
Without your insanity,
Nothing ever felt so detached and artificial,
Copy paste, love is something that you didn't pass on,
Didn't convey, you never received it in the first place.

And I feel your empty hands on me
And I want to set them on fire.

You have always felt like an emptying threat to me.
Shooting your insults and bile into my body
When you should have kept your mouth shut.

Taking these grand emotions into your mouth,
Your daily vocabulary, your act, the pseudo-grandeur,
Without backing them up with actions, with truth,
You don't know what they feel like and you pretended
Because you needed, you told me lies because
You wanted to appease and manipulate me into your arms,
Again and again, and I let myself be devoured,
Let myself be drowned in your endless monologues
And you took every piece of me for granted,
Portraying yourself as both the hero and the victim
And every time I told you how you made me feel inside

You looked away in disbelief, as if I hadn't said a thing.

Your attention is a roaring multi-faced beast,
    unpredictable and volatile,
The worst kind of absence, the worst kind of presence.
You've made yourself known.

Everybody I ask tells me the same lies, weaves the same
    romantic
Picture of who my father was.

And I can see them swallowing their own pain,
Their own truths like fire,
Casual self-betrayal, deep wrinkles carved into their skin.

I stood by you as a child
When I would have needed a father
Who protected me instead of exposing me,
Consuming me,
Draining me
And terrorising me into his unnatural embrace.

The Child Can Speak | A Poem, On Two Feet

And I felt you watch me.
You waited for my decomposition.
You took part in it, directed it
And yet, despite all of your efforts,
I stood up with bruises on my knees
And broken bones and a heart that skipped beats,
And succeeded, I found refuge within me,
Found revolt in my body, found my voice
In my spirit, I didn't abandon myself in the darkness
You shoved me into.

You wanted me to endure what you endured,
Live in constant pain and fury and disappointment.
You made sure of that every step of the way.
Neglect, carelessness, lack of everything.
And you resent me for overcoming your obstacles,
For making it through your hurdles, your minefield,
For coming out of you alive and with a sense of humour,
That's the worst part, isn't it?

That I can still laugh without faking it?
Everything I had to outweigh your body and your silence
Was my language, I speak, Father, I am language,
My body is language and I open my mouth to finally have
    my say
And regurgitate what you made me swallow.
Set you free, set myself free,

Rid myself of lessons taught,
You taught me one thing, I learned another.
You wanted me quiet and submissive.
Your unbuckled belt wavering,
Oh, you know better than to beat me,
Don't you, I've taught you not to,
At some point your hands came across fire
When they approached my body, but you have always been
    resourceful
And slithered into my head.
I depended on you and you loved it.

You, the provider and withdrawer of goods,
You honoured yourself with a sizzling neon halo
And I wait for you by the side of the road.

I see you in men who pull their cocks out.
Reveal themselves to anyone who smiles.
You taught me not to smile.

Not to look at men, at boys, because then they
Would think that I wanted them, that my face was an
    open
Invitation, subject object, you turn everything on its head,
Right, Father, everything turned around,
Everything I did, I wanted, I initiated,
I was to blame and shame, *walk all over me, this is what you
    get.*

I was asked to play an adult when I was a girl
And take responsibility for *my* actions and shortcomings.
(I looked like an adult, I looked like a doll,
But I could not have been younger inside)
And I did respond to you as a child.
Where did I come from, Father?

Are you not holding my roots in your hands?

You washed yourself shameless and I was kneeling below
   you
With my mouth open, receiving your sins, receiving your
   vices.
Devilchild, deranged girl, *she needs to see someone,*
She's not normal, you escaped, and I was painted scarlet
   red.

I acted the way you taught me and you withdrew your
   authorship
In the open light where everyone could be fooled.
That's what you're so good at, fooling everyone who claims
To adore you and who you mock and judge relentlessly.

They don't get that you're a trap,
That you gorge and prey with a frightening appetite,
That you take what you don't deserve until you're full
For a moment and we are all empty, dreading nightfall.

Fatherfiguregirls | A Midnight Poem

As a young girl I saw everything.
Of you.
Every terrifying bit, overpowering.
I've studied you, the pretentious saint,
The capabilities of *man*,
The actor and director, the limelight
On your face and hands. What your body
Did overtly, in hidden corners, around midnight.

Your lips on my cheeks, I barely remember them.
The man who wanders through the night, through women,
Through me as a child, I don't know who my father is
And I know all too well.
You think that I'm harmless – because you made sure that
    I had no boundaries-
I showed you my injuries and you played the saviour – *told*
    you so, you're too weak –
And you whispered in my ear that I have to bite
If I want to survive, if I want to live,
There was no difference for you, and you nibbled and I was
    blind,
The world was out to get you and I had to pity you, – you
    loved my empathy –
And you nurtured and harvested a blind audience
And you wanted me to trust your empty words
But I was looking at your forked tongue instead and
    realised that

I was born with my fists out
Against you.

And yes, there were times when
I ended up begging for some form of love
Because I was so tired from fighting you off, keeping you at bay,
Walking on eggshells with the weight of an inflammable thick skin.

She lives in her own world.
She has too vivid an imagination.
(Why would you not see? Why would you not listen?)
Unrelatable, unbelievable, unheard of.
I created my own language to survive and checkmate you.
Because you never said a word.

You created worlds that nobody could see,
That everybody denied existed,
That have been there since the dawn of time,
And I was born as you put yourself in me, in her,
Pieces of you that I will never get to know,
Revealing themselves to me as I'm pushed over the edge,
Becoming man, becoming animal, becoming hungry for blood,
As a child from your flesh, I give you pieces of me
To keep myself alive and nobody ever acknowledges them
And you prance with my blood wounds as decorations on your open-mouthed head,
The laurels of my spine, my childhood, and you keep denying what you took.

That you gave me the worst of your world
And I gave you the best of mine.

You threatened us with images of your death,
Omnipresent, and you'd make us responsible,
And preached that we shouldn't dare mourn,
That it would be on us, you infiltrated our hearts
And plagued us with suicide exclamations and we swallowed
A guilt that did not belong to us.

You splashed blood on our walls, used your evoked death against us
Throughout your whole life and yet fought and raged against
The end of your life, because you hold on with all the power you have left, don't you?

Hold on to us, to us children, because we gave you life
And called our sacrifices yours, over and over again,
Blaming us for being alive and draining us remorselessly.

And we sought father figures in familiar devils,
Legs open wide, chin up, *look into my eyes*. Is this me? Is this you?
(Doesn't it sound too familiar?)
You devoured my childhood.
Hands on me when I'm on my knees.
I'm scared to death but my mouth's wide open.
You split my soul and I collapse within myself.
And I keep offering and offering my body to the father figure(s) that failed me.

And now I am taking back the pieces of my soul,
Even broken glass is still transparent and reveals the original mould.
Because you know, Father, that I,
My mother's daughter, am anything but harmless.

That's Not How You Say My Name | Out Of Your Mouth | Thievery In The Name Of The Father

Childhood is a voice that I'm unburying until my vocal cords hurt.
*
Memory is a companion who leaves me hanging in a labyrinth.
*
The past is a cemetery with bells and drums and without bodies.
*
The bedroom that I grew up in collapses beneath the weight of What it still contains when I look back into it.
*
We lost one another.
*
The window in my mother's bathroom – it's not hers anymore –
Still frames my neck with its trafficked air, the scent of the garden, clutching,
Dreams that I sent out into the wilderness through a guillotine.
*
My grandfather's urn still stares at me, begs me from the chest of drawers,
Containing the things that survived the owner, sombre and affectionate.

*
The basement which frightened me, its yellow wet heavy odour,
Where my clothes get washed, where reminiscence makes the air smell familiar,
The promise of pain hammered into my brain, on paper, on a door,
In transition, punishment awaiting, my bones, the tunnel of misfortunes,
The war in a body, divorced from history, the room full of letters,
The room full of useful instruments and obsolete decorations,
I still run up the stairs into someone's arms.
*
Doors which the wind slammed shut, the sensation my (grand)father left behind,
Heart tightly shut, overfired, overburdened, fury, shut, *run away*,
The sound warns me, there will be consequences, someone grabs
The object now, as I prepare myself, as I write, now, someone is getting ready
To chase me around, reliving the war, the female form is eroded by escapist tendencies.

My body, my presence, make it burst, bring it out, the compartmentalised inner truths.

Men rubbing against me. Men trying to rid my lungs of air.
I am trying to understand who they are. What they want. From me.

And I give them everything.
Every single piece of my body that does the trick.

That saves me. That satisfies them. And I bleed and cannot
    cover up the orchestral wounds.
That were demanded, that I seemed to offer, that I thought
    were necessary,
Natural, what girls do, what children do, what your
    (grand)daughters do,
To save themselves, save you, each and every day anew, the
    adult tongue,
Hands on you, hands on me, eyes on me, I saw your
    projections in my own head
And played the part with a broken heart.

A fragment of my spirit, on my knees I bring myself back
    together
Because you spit me out, my belongings, you absorb them,
    reject them,
And I am beneath you with my mouth open, hands eager
    to recollect,
Rebuild, I always did, I always re-erected myself, under
    your regime,
And you put your desires and wishes in-between my lips
And I swallowed death and the way you abused my name
    and
What it stood for before you tarnished it.

Hands Off | Mind Off | Turn Off

I can't find my own words anymore.
You hear what you want.
All words are scarlet red, dirty, burdened.
You've lost all nuances.

Language is ice that breaks beneath our feet.

I can't say it. You can't say it.
What are you saying?
Is that what you're thinking?
Guillotine, end of dialogue, monologue against monologue.
Hands on my feet.

I build a world in my bedroom.

Can't listen to you. Can't think.
Can't feel. Overwhelmed. Land in flames and words.
Spikes and cotton wool.
Vocabulary without life, without substance.
But you have motifs. You have intentions.
Parrot, echo, copy, repeat, circles, recycling, all voices mutate into one.
You have no idea who you are and why you kneel and repeat.
I need to care about this.
I need to show that I care, care with my fingertips, I care, I care,

I care, can't you see? Did I not yell loud enough?
Never enough, never sufficient, feed me blindly.
Self-importance, smaller picture, rhetoric, suffocation,
   right, right, righteous.

What is going on behind your face?

Language is a minefield, syntax, meaningful,
   misunderstand me,
Misinterpret me, decontextualise me, dehumanise me,
Rid me of sense, strip me of what I intended,
Create what you wanted to hear,
Paint me in red, showcase everything wrong in your eyes,
Focus on the unfortunate details and leave the human
   package behind,
No softener for your hardcore stance, imagination,
   projection.

You want to sell me something.

I'm not buying it, not playing along,
It bores me to sit in a corner facing your shrinking walls.

Fatherjaw | Daughterfist

What's the matter with that child?
Put your hands on me, put your words on me.
Layer after layer, lie after lie, embodying love
In all its failures and shortcomings.

It wasn't love, was it? It wasn't you, was it?

Nobody's fault, nobody's responsibility,
What's wrong with that child?

Your lips on my cheeks, the violence in your rustling
 throat.
Stubs on your face irritating my skin.
Little bitch, little bitch, behave, don't be such a tease,
Just a little bit, just all the way, just this, just that,
I like this, I like that, come on now, what is it going to be?

Men's voices across my ages. I was taught to expect the
 worst.
I looked to women for kindness. They hurt me more. And
 I did, too.
Can't you tell, can't you tell at all?
Sitting on laps, I embody an insult.
I am my father's disappointment personified.
His eyes follow me when I am falling apart.
He appears then and there.
Attention seeks its selected moments.

That's when he tries to see.
That's when he chisels and threatens and pokes and rages.
I am my father's rebuckled belt.
I have no use for it.

Who told you to undress, to derail, to escalate, to spit fire in my face?
Eat, go on, eat, shove it all in, in it goes, fill yourself up,
Is it enough yet, you want more, and more, and I pay and pay for it.
Do you know what boys would do to you?
Can you imagine?

You taught me everything I wished to forget.

I listened and bathed in the misery you put on me like garments.
I teach myself to disregard the good.
I teach myself to disregard the bad.
You'd still say the same things.
You'd still scream and curse the world.
You'd still not see the point in me.
You'd still perform and pretend to love to use me well.
Maybe there is some truth in you,
I wish that I could find it.

Fathertongue | Daughtererasure

You built a house and filled it with death images.

Memories that were none.
You evoked an atmosphere that branded itself into my brain.

I was born into the horror of your words.

You spoke to me as a personal possession.
About me as if I were of no use, as if I'd never matter, but you were sucking.
I waited for you most of my life, abandoned and neglected,
You'd forget me, you didn't care, and I thought *I'll never make it home.*

You planted sentences in my head that I'd never forget
Or rid myself of.
You cursed the existence of my body.
The hunger within me, the lack I suffered.

You dragged me along the same destitute street that you knew so well.
Shoving my face into the dirt, *teaching me, teaching me.*

Love, it never sounded right.
Your mouth sounds wrong.

Your touch, as rarely as it comes, all wrong.
Dishonest, ill-intentioned, draining, in need, bloodthirsty.
You took and took and mocked me still, denied my worth,
And I kept feeding you, myself, listening to your language
Used against me, weaponised fatherhood,
Love is a head-hunter, a curse on my shoulders, in the home you built.

Transferral Of Trauma | In Good Faith

I grew up in the confinement of your rage.

Adapted to it, trying to prevent it, contain it,
Hide myself away once I realised that I
Embodied a catalyst for it.
You robbed me of protection.
You exposed me and walked away from
Your acts of negligence.
I never managed to stand firmly on my own two feet.

I took part in the wars that waged inside of you.
To feel closer to you, to connect with you.
Stand by your side.
You gorged on the attention I offered you.
You'd never be satisfied, your suffering was endless.
I needed to be endless.

My childhood cure. The medicinal daughter.
I listened to your mental illness.
To your insults and abuse until I burst
And promised myself that you won't make anything out of me anymore.

I wouldn't put anything into your hands anymore.
Nothing that belonged to me.

I made fun of you to weaken my fears.
And nobody would believe how dangerous you were.
He is who he is. And I would parody you behind your back to stop crying.

No matter what I'd do you'd be outraged, disgusted, revolted.
So be it. You begged for my life to live it yourself.
And you watched me disintegrate in my teens
In service to you.

The violence you spread to make everything collapse around me
As you were screaming about death and non-forgiveness.

I grew old as a child in a house where I had to fight for my life.

And you labelled it love and care, the rage-distorted face pecking at my skin,
You told me to trust your never-ending baptism by fire.

Anticipation / Deterioration

I am all bodies at once.
I stem from a cacophony of bodies.
The wounds of my mother.
The silence of my grandmother.
The broken heart of my great-grandmother.

I'll bring you all down in a heartbeat, the act of so-called love, transgressive conceptions.

And I'd inherit the sense of powerlessness that my father caused.
The lines that my grandfather's addiction and warhead crossed.
The love my great-grandfather extracted from his child(ren) because he was in need.

(If love is not given freely, you do not take it)

You shoved me into that room of voices.
They were bursting.
There were no signs.
You fed them to me bit by bit.
You eat. You become them. We do.
We watched one another dissolve.
Under the pressure. The heat.
The relentless expectations.
I chewed and used my muscles to get rid of everything.

And there were no more boundaries.
We all became alike, sucked in, torn and twisted.
Fork chasing knife, hands with fingers that fight.
Mind over matter, a body attached to body after body
After life and death.
You spoke to me with your pretentious body.
I knew your words inside out.
Red on my skin, blatant, combustible, etched in,
Arrow after arrow, tense and straightforward.

You used an idea of love to destroy it.

Preying, in circles, I collapse under your weight.
And you ingest my scent claiming that it is not mine.
Man-made, eliminate, anatomy, singalong, digestive,
   endorsed.

I sit in the corner of a room calling all the dead
That you acquainted me with, my body knows them too
   well
For my own taste.

Nothing Made You Feel Better Than Girls Betraying Each Other For Your Attention

My father made sure that I'd look for him everywhere.
You made sure that I'd find him in you.
I had already had enough and yet I projected myself onto you
In false hope, with false hands, false mouth, false voice.

Our bodies were not a coincidence.
I tried on what became of me,
I spoke according to my impaled stuck appetite,
My loneliness.
I was taught to be extreme, to push, to bring out and resonate with
Everything men hide within themselves.
Tune out of my own body.
And they single me out immediately.
I learned that as a child.
They'd seek me out in darkness
Because they're ashamed yet needy.
In darkness, they take without asking.
They think that we're on the same page.
No, they wrote the book and I was a blank page.

We never spoke the same language.
You revealed yourself to me and I was not aware that I played a part.

I escaped into something, made it pretty, something you
    expected from me.
I come to you to see my father walk away again and again.
I come to you to reclaim intimacy and let the devil into my
    body.
But I am not a daughter in your grip.
I become someone that I don't own, but I think I do, that's
    the trick.
The original lie, *that this is what I want, what I initiate; this
is who I truly am.*

I internalised the expectations of your body.
I was taught that all men are irresistible
And that I had obligations.
I watched men plunder and ransack the bodies of women.

Driving around, insatiably stopping to eat women alive.
Pressure them out of their clothes.
And they'd smile in a tired way, *just get it over with then.*
Men who'd pester women until they'd give in
So that they could finally get rid of them.

And you'd parade their hearts around in slander,
And woman would turn against woman,
You put all your money on the power of jealousy.

They thought they needed you inside of them
Becoming embodiments of heartache.
But you abandoned their bodies with your poison inside of
    them all.
You proclaimed your love of women
As if you were selling body parts at a butcher's.

Your misogyny disguised as lust,
As appetite, as love, and you fucked and plucked and drained,

All of them into you, you ate them all up, misanthropic underwhelmed gulps.
They kissed you and felt their soul disengage,
Something had never been right, they all stormed into a wrong premise
And leapt blindly into all the steps that you had laid out for them already.

Deprivation / Embrace / Toxicity | From Your Body Into Every Letter

Insanity, eyes closed, *I feel you still*, tightly shut, mouth,
Listen to me, I can't speak,
You don't want me to,
You don't want to hear me,
You say that I have no voice and hug me with your sickness.

I smell your skin around my face,
Drunk, cactus, rubbing, you hurt.
My body is not strong enough yet.
(Or was I so strong from the beginning
That you thought, *she can bear it, she can take it. (?)*
I (she) can carry a man's body, a man's desires as a girl. (?)
I (she) can hold his (my) thoughts on my (her) skin. (?)
And let them in. (?) Let them sink into my (her) flesh. (?))
Did I not inherit that moulded female body?
Am I a supplierchild?
Do you see how twisted and intertwined we became?
Yellow, that's the scent, your taste, on me.
Tongue, wasteland, hollow me out, wood.

Echoes amidst the dust of our home,
Holding me, steps following me around, I'm quiet.
Fill me up, your innate burdens, on my shoulders,
Down and down I wander, wondering *where am I coming from*,
Feeling you, everything of you, in fragments

And pieces, syringes, cutting into me, the skin *she* developed,
The skin I've been put into and you were ever-hungry.

Looking at me, eyes on flesh, clothes disappearing, voice lost.
I had a strong voice and you know it,
Swallowed it and I ate you alive to get it back.

The Truth In Your Lies | Fatherdaughterface

I tasted my own braid in my throat.
You urged me to be satisfied.
My voice split in two, distorted, drying out,
You wanted to hear yourself talk amidst my self-murdering silence.
You never liked what I had to say, what I saw, you do.

You separated us. We were born into a different world.
You penetrated our world with wars and hammers
And relentless chicanery. I hear your words when I eat.

You're indigestible.
I don't want to swallow and internalise your voice.
Make it part of myself. It doesn't belong here.
Can I even say *no*? I *owe* you my life.
Isn't that what you're still holding against me?

Every bite, every taste, from me to you, is yours,
I was born indebted to you.
Since I could breathe you've taken from me.

You imposed. I was yours. And I learned.
I was alive in your house and you'd made *all the sacrifices*.
You'd never let me forget.

You denied the existence of monsters yet you kept growing.

If you have ever been someone that I could relate to,
We were not alive at the same time.
Maybe at one point, we would have made sense, together,
And then everything was too late.
Something didn't survive.
Something was overpowering, misdirected.

(All of your *sacrifices* became my responsibility at birth)

I became a *daughter neglected* as you rejected yourself
    within me.
You called me ugly before you put your hands on me
    (confessed your love to me?)
And it has always felt like a sin, like a lie, that you told
    yourself
To counteract your fear of death.

Womansilhouette / Fathertantrum / Wardrumchemistry

Mother's underarm, his finger above the ashtray.
Tipping point, standstill, jaw tight, eyes on her.
Counting your sins and mistakes.
Back and forth. Clenched, doorknob, heat on his skin.

Siblingcall, ancestry, branches breaking in two.
Motherlode, hiding you in wardrobes.
Doing what I feel. Doing what I saw.
Doing what I was taught.

Am I alive?
Am I, in your arms?

Coffee stains, butter knife, stuck, skin, melting.
Sinking into books, fortresses, hair, grip, *inhale me*.

I surrendered. I broke. I scratched and hollered my way back up.
Spine, pastry, pulverised, sugar on my tongue, fork hunting fingernail.
I sing, your fist on my door, keys in my hand, the hole is mine.
The past of our bodies shows up again and again,
The ghosts of our skins, the shadows of our ancestral patterns.

I turn and turn, pirouette, figured myself out, hands off.

I played with the ruins you left me in.
Didn't I have fun?
Was that the tragedy?
That I started laughing?
That I saw things that you didn't?
Sullied, back, hips, hair, oh,
You were a lost cause and I'd make my way out of there.

Running after me, what is wrong with you,
What were you thinking, knocking, knocking,
I shut you out, shaved my skin, head out of the window.
I became your echo.
You saw yourself. In me.
Trashed yourself into me.
Now listen to yourself.

Knock knock, salt, eyeballs, strength on my tongue,
I split you in half in my mouth, listen to me now.

I don't need you to. I'm not on my knees anymore.
Feet above our burial ground, pans across the room,
Teeth, children with invisible wounds, to the bone,
    knuckles in my memory,
Chin high, elbow tight, hair up, stop your ludicrous
    fantasy.

Girlspine / Daughterendurance / *Father Maniacal*

You watched me grow with a violent face.
Standing in my way, biting your tongue.
Restraining yourself, the tense muscles.
I felt your eyes on me, your insistent judgement.
Your disapproval. A vulture locking
Its teeth around its offspring.

I remember the mockery in the angle of your mouth.
The glistening gaze, transferring pain.
From your body into mine.
I moved and you fired.

And as we were running away from your predictable
    outbursts
Or hiding somewhere or giving in or raising our fists
To protect ourselves, you still had the nerve
To perform your self-victimisation,
Calling us names, pointing your fingers,
Cursing us, burdening us with your crimes and abuses.
I lived in your house of madness.
(*I don't know what you are talking about. We are just talking.
    Just, Just, Just.*)

Amongst the ghosts that your body produced.
Alongside past selves of mine that I buried over the years.

Skins shed too early, constantly, renewed, because I had to survive you.
I had to grow, outgrow, adapt to your tempers and insanity.
Learn the steps of the dysfunctional dance.
I slept in a bed of dead selves, holding on, mourning, constantly.
Never reaching who I was.

All I was forced to do was fight you, keep you at bay.
And I changed several times a day.

You drained me and recharged yourself.
You made me so that I could feed you.
You wanted someone to starve for you.
Someone else to keep you alive.
Someone else responsible for your life.
No matter how many souldeaths you'd cause.

Heartland / Whispers White

I didn't know that you gave names to wounds.
A book of memories in your hands.
The tip of your tongue, list of insults.
In the back of your head, the rhythm of your heartbeat
Where voices meet and interact, infecting the one true
  thing.
I didn't know that you paved a path
Between life and death with everything that hurts.

I didn't acknowledge your daily steps on the reimagined
  homeland.
Are you still looking for something?
How many pieces did they take away?
Something that was given to you and then stolen?
Is your vocabulary a puzzle that you were forced to put
  together?
Did it make you who you are?
Did it create the time you live in now?

The dead kept themselves alive, didn't they?
Or did you?
Did they suddenly start to talk?
And tell you the truth?
And how could you ever heal if they remain sick to the
  bone?
Integrated in your body.

And you'd lose all the blood.

Who did you focus on?
Who gained your attention?
Were you followed?
I look at you.
I look at me and thoughts collide.

Names collide. Paths are intertwined.
We were born without choreographies amidst a cacophony
    of dancing warfeet.

Ashwaterdaughter / Daughterhair | Self-exorcism

Your disgust was never without appetite.
Your eyes gleamed with all shades of guilt
And endless stings of reproach.
For something done and unravelled.
My body, perhaps, our bodies,
Our names that we wouldn't live up to,
What went on inside of your head.

I could never figure it out,
Put it on the full map,
Decipher the landscapes of your insanity.
You dragged me into your footsteps
Until I became submissive,
Until I did everything to accompany you,
To keep you calm,
To avoid unnecessary violence,
Exaggerated outbursts, the outlines expanding into
    limitlessness.

Daughterhair, oh mine,
Oh yours,
To pull, to harass, afire, ashwater, sinkhead,
I begged you without words,
When all I had left was to stand on my feet
With fists ready to go,
When fury meets explosion,
We meet each other there,
You made me go there,

Daddy animalistic, survival mode,
Body protective, sense of self,
Vampiredaddy sucks my soul out,
Blood staining his teeth.

Girlmouth / Fathertwig / Daughterporcelain

I hear that you don't like the words coming out of my mouth.
The sounds a child makes that belongs to you.

You own. You don't borrow. You take and possess.
Your body turned our home into a straitjacket.
Torment in the rhythm of neglect.
Combustion in the form of projection.
Hands on me, hands on yourself.

Self-loathing straight onto my body.
My hair in your limelight.
My eyes in your prison cell.
My resentment gasoline under your roof, my roof.
Cut into one another.
You strained the boundaries of my body.
Erected an altar to yourself in my head.

And I lost sight of my hands, my thighs, my heart.
Lost touch, gained yours, theirs, violence, poisoned sentences.

Absence and presence deformed into one and the same thing.
Past and present. You held me. Vigil.

An avid candle flickering too close to the strands of my hair.

Dyed, volatile, cover-up, close-up, away from you, colour
  first.
I swallowed your images.
The never-ending narratives you preach past midnight.

Starlight, flight of stairs, slippers, stomping, memory, mine.
Aggravated heartbeat, child, body, man, lifetime horrors
Glued to the underground matter of your skin(s).

Coming at me, full throttle, energy afire, ever-developing
  balloons,
Squeezing, tighter, anticipation, hide-and-seek,
Find-me-not, we are a knot, disentangle me.

Daughtermouth | Daddyruins

Daddy, Daddy, needs you.
Daddy, asked too much,
Everything, Daddy does.

Wants, always, never enough, wrinkles,
Daddy sounds mad, all the time,
I'm guilty, I haven't said a word,
Never knew what I did, Daddy screams,
He runs so fast, lives in another world,
Everyone applauds, laurels on his head.

What is going on, bad bad girl, Daddy, gave me
No speech, Daddy didn't teach me his language,
And they love him so hard, women swallow him,
One after another, men emulate Daddy.

I look at the women, grab the wrong shoes to
To step in. Daddy, Daddy mistreats them all,
With his mouth, his silver tongue,
I hear the way Daddy talks about women behind
Their backs. Who will *I* become?

Daddy's mouth has no trace of love.
He mocks. He salivates. He eats them all.
Daddy does. His desire is violent.
And they run after him.
I want to flee.

As far away as possible.
Daddy escaped, too.
He never said why.
He'd lie.
We picked out the stories.

A land containing all of his secrets.
Mistakes.
Crimes.
Who knows.
I observe Daddy.
I know when to hide.
When to use my key.
When to run.
When to face the monsters within him.
When to overcome my fear and raise my chin.

Daddy doesn't like rebellion in his house.
Daddy uses and hates his own face.
And mine.
He tries to destroy his in mine.
Mine instead.
From within.

He pretends to love.
He pretends.
What do I know?
He left me in the shadows.
But that's where Daddy lives, too.
And you don't know it.
You don't see it.
Daddy needs everything.
More and more.
Daddy is a little boy.
He takes what he needs.

And I look at this grown body
And wish to outgrow mine immediately.

But that's what the way Daddy talks does,
And I became old very quickly,
Remembering the women Daddy seemed to adore,
And I learned that he emptied them all, too late,
That they meant nothing, (too late)
And absolutely everything.

Daughtertongue | Swallow

I taught myself how to read
The way your body moves,
How you behave,
What the sound of your voice meant.
You instilled doubt.
I was born truthful.
And you saw an opening.
And you stuffed the vulnerable,
Expanded nothingness.

It belonged to you.
I grew up within it.
You left it with me.
And it told me all the wrong things.
I enabled it to grow
As I started shrinking alongside it.
Was that your plan?
Absorbing every single piece of me?
Stopping me?

Telling me that I was talentless?
That I would never be good enough?
It happens so often
It has become a cliché.
Acceptable.
The way you put me down.
The way fathers put down girls.

Everything it means,
How the slow violence travels,
Long lengths, following me,
Sometimes I barely remember your voice.
It left first.

But, there are moments,
When it comes back and I feel it
In my bones,
In my tense muscles,
Contracted, trying to rebuild my armour,
Trying to become a grown-up as a girl,
Who is afraid of her own father.

You came too close and
I saw too much,
Heard too much,
Felt too much,
Everything you unleashed
And burdened me with,
And yet the weight never shrank,
You'd never rid yourself of
Your demons and cursed
Me for your sleepless poison red temper.

Aren't You Full Yet? | All I Could Think About

I took you in
And I believed that
I had to become like you
With all the things that I wasn't,
That I didn't have
And I merely focused
On everything
That was negating who I was
In opposition to you.

I let myself fail and fail
And never learn,
I taught myself a lack of solace,
A continuous self-abuse,
Hearing those voices again,
Negating everything,
Disengaging with my intuition,
And I slept within the skins of madness and jealousy,
Thinking I would never find myself,
I would never find out
Who I was
And what I could do.

You loved that,
You held my hair upright
And paraded my body in the sick admiration
I nurtured for you,

The compliments you inhaled,
My entire vocabulary, my misguided love
On a silver platter
And you'd cut into me,
I exposed myself to you
And you fed yourself to death.

Always wanting, needing, forcing more
Out of me, of me,
Until I heard my own name (the one you gave me)
Ring false in your throat.

The Apple Came
With Maggots All Along

You thought of me
As your possession.
A body to cure yours.
A soul to stand by you
No matter what,
No matter how hard you hit
No matter how infuriating you were
No matter how much you neglected me,
I had to persist.

Be there on all fours.

Yes, it's a repetitive scheme,
The monologues I listened to
And drowned in,
You loved it,
My participation in your theatrics,
My crumbling beneath you.

And you pushed that foot on the pedal
And I thought, *I will die*,
He is going to kill his own daughter,
I thought about opening that door,
A car racing like his pulse,
I thought I'd be safer jumping out,
Landing in some hedge beside the road,

Walking, running home, bruised, a cut or two, but still
    alive at least,
And he'd find me again. (How did we live like that for so
    long?)

Your speeches were never over,
He, you, he, you,
Everything became you,
That's what you wanted, right?
Survive at all costs.

And I started exiling myself, condemning places,
Condemning people, exorcising
The discarded traces of your life in mine.

The energy of our history lingers.
We still bring it to the table.
In the abandoned houses, in our bodies.
She put everything into those family albums
So that we could forget everything that also happened
Behind the snapshots of our lives
And she truly meant well.
And they truly looked good.
Until the scales tipped and the albums stopped.

Eruption / Destruction / Evocation / Recreation | A Poem Despite All Of Your Efforts

Everything dissolved
Slowly
Achingly
Kisses on gravestones, butter,
Lips dry on your skin
Enveloped
Lies across your face, onto mine.

Bodies revealing truths,
Taking me aside,
Thinking I was special,
Solitude,
Trust,
Why?

Too young.
Too carefree.
Unloading
You(rself)
Unloaded
Everything.

Your knives in my hair.
Masks protected me.
You saw everything.

Encircled
Hands
Formed
Shadows around my face.

Scum, you hid it,
In plain sight,
The traces,
I swallowed them,
Integrated you,
Bit by bit,
Dancing in a fire,
Shedding skin after skin after skin
Barely old enough to count
Your flaws
And crimes
And lies and salt in the name of love.

Teaching me
What you learned,
Our bodies were supposed to be the same.
Suffer the same things
And your shame,
Your rage
Became my own
And I vanished.

Found a little hellhole within me.

You took over
My entire body
And nothing was ever good enough.

And I grew old
As a child

Old as a daughter
Assembling all my inner children
That you wanted lost and never found,
And
Oh, I have found them all
And raised them against you.

You've made my bed and
I torched it to the ground.

Dragging In An Audience | Taking Part In Your Mental Illness

I sat in your sickness,
You watched my birth
And wanted to attach
Me to your body.

You faked love.

You looked at her.
Sullied every piece of
My mother tongue.
Offering nothing in return.

Looked at the flaws
Of her body, of mine,
Ignored how our lungs filled with air
How our mouths spoke and formed words
How we could run and laugh.

None of it mattered to you,
Health didn't matter.
Women's heads in the kitchen sink.

Your hands wanting to hurt,
To cross lines, but then she started to
Look beautiful to you, too pretty to destroy.
You turned to the duplication of your face instead.
The one grimacing at me right now,

The degeneration of your language
That had only been present through curses and wrath
And endless scenes of bitterness and violence.

You hunted yourself instead.
Beat yourself, beat him, and me, and him,
Instead, your own face, what you saw in us,
What you wanted gone within yourself,
And I tried to give birth to myself again
And again and again, shutting you out,
The wounds on my *body memorial*,
The words hammering against my skull.

And I spoke to myself, *you have to get out of here*, you'll get out of here,
Out of his sickness, I could barely breathe,
Your hands, your voice, your steps were everywhere,
In the house we built and you contaminated
Every single wall that watched silently,
The walls that masterminded her depression, everything
Just kept growing and nobody would listen
Because I never forgot how to smile,
So how on earth could life be that bad?

In Rejection Of Your Saints | Tell Them Yourself

Muscle mass, swampland, crucifix, chokehold, eyes pop,
Love burns, fingernails, butter, smokescreen,
Wives in silence, head of the table, substitute, compost,
Swallowed voices, candlelight, rings on wood,
Aging wine, my lips, childhood, singalong,
Spell my name, screaming into blankets,
Churning, exposed, stomach, touch, touched,
Everlasting, mattress-faced, illusions of my face,
Amongst you, your body mass, hair, foreign, on my skin,
Old child, *girl come to me, on me, closer, here,* fed,
Open up, I teach you words, and I die and I die,
Longing, sandbox, thornbath, listen, never, yellow,
Stains, burning, spine, crawling along, withdrawal,
What is wrong with her, so shy, tickling, ticking,
Exasperating, do what I want, what I need, fuckface,
    compliment,
Provide, feed me, feel my heartbeat, watching me grow up,
Up, up, up, jump on me, arrest the moment, my body,
Everything is always about sex, slapped into my face,
You taught me, on repeat, on repeat, singalong,
    sexualisation,
Stretch and touch and kneel, comfort is a trap called
    home.

You can't go anywhere, I set your roof on fire,
I created a tomb for the living,
All I see is death, on your fingertips,

In my mouth, sucking, regurgitated, shredded by you,
And I sit on a wall,
My legs dangling, hot air, a sandwich collapsed,
I tore it apart, I never found a heart.
I
Never
Found
A
Heart.

Keeping Your Gargoyles At Bay | You Told Me To Be Silent | Walking Through Marshlands

You looked
At me
With an
Open mouth.
I know your teeth
Inside out.
I fed myself.

Everything happened in your name.
When would it become mine?
Something that I could call mine?
My body?

Yours to play with, deform, manipulate and curse.
Sending me into arms
And fondling hands
Afire
Acidic
That hurt
And tore apart with lying caresses
Drooling tongues
Saying prayers
In unfamiliar languages.
For your sake.

Appetite.
I grew,
Inwards, backwards,
Around every single finger of yours,
The extremities of your friends,
Everything
Was wrong with me –
What –
What then?

A Phantom On Its Knees

I was a girl
And you touched what you wanted me to bury.

I buried and
Buried,
Flesh over flesh,
Skin on skin,
Kilogram over kilogram,
Womanhood over girlhood,
Childhood, buried,
Strings around your fingernails,
You defined and polluted what I would have become.

You spoke to me in secretive gestures and glances,
Letting me know,
Letting me take part,
Letting me perform,
Letting me relate to,
Letting me embody the images in your head,
Making me aware of you, not me,
I lie here, buried,
And you play with me, robbing me of my senses,
And I detach myself from my body and unlearn the word
 no.

I put layers and layers
Of myself

On myself
Over myself
To not feel you anymore
To not let you in anymore
To feel less of
You.

Shut you out,
Myself, as well,
And still, I'd be a feather in a raging wind.

Push and pull
And I'd still end up in your arms.
I'd eat myself into protection,
I wanted,
Needed, thicker skin.

Recreating bits and pieces without your pestilent touch,
Stuffing, numbing, feeding
The void you tore into my body,
As if nothing of me was left,
A heart beating into nothingness,
Becoming your repetitive confessional box and torture
    chamber.
You were growing in my hands
In my spine,
In my skin,
Hands, thighs, mouth and hair,
You wanted to survive within me,
But I finally look like myself now and smoked you out.

Down Your Throat My Language Goes | Rub Your Face In It

I tried finding
Love
In the body
Called Father.

I tried finding
Everything
Fatherly
In your body
Language.

The act of
Your body
And mine
Against mine.

All bodies fatherly
Rubbing against mine,
Into corners,
Into survival mode,
Screaming matches,
Running away from each other's minds.

You buried your past
And fought with your dead.
They lived in our house.
They told me what to do.

You shoved your voice down my throat.
On my knees.
And I ran,
Ran away in my mind,
Standing still, talking to shadows,
Holding on,
The key in my door.

Your mouth at the keyhole.

Whispers, on your knees,
I've always had enough,
Of you,
The sound of you,
The violence,
The stampede of dialect,
The absence of language,
Love abused, love overused, love inexistent.

You needed and needed and drank and got drunk
With me on all fours, gagging, holding myself together
To not shatter
Under your weight.

You broke and built
According to the sick world in your head.
I didn't correspond.
I blew myself up
And apart,
It has never been me.
Not in your arms,
Yours,
Never,
Yours,
The animal within,

The dead within,
The ghosts singing songs that I have never heard,
Never known.

The words in my bones,
The fork in your hand,
The blade in-between my lips,
Count your sins,
Embody yourself.

I've crawled out of the confessional box
With my hands clean,
Of you and what you've thought of me
Since you created me.

Drained / Exit Wound

I write you down
Before I don't remember you anymore.

Write you out
Of my skin
Before dust settles in.

I stared at your footsteps
And invented my own.

You abused the beauty of your voice.
It has never forgiven you.
For everything you made it say and turning it into something ugly.

You shrank and dissolved without telling me who you really were.

You haunted my childhood.
Your homecomings and goings,
The smells you brought with you.
I closed my eyes because I thought it would protect me.

What did you want from me?
Your life back? Life itself?
Everything before and after I was born and you let go?
What about the lives you created?

In your eyes, we were the opposite of your life.
And you led your multiple lives and created us so that we'd
 finance them.

Your flaws and crimes and lies exhausted me.
Every time I thought that I knew who my father was
You blew yourself out of proportion again and violated
Your predictability.

Telling me all the things that I do wrong
All the things that you never taught me at all.
Nothing's ever right.

You cling like a child and lean on me like a scolded god
When I had just learned how to walk.

You robbed me of my language before I could speak.

I didn't deserve your language, all I got was your
 guttertongue.

Poison Ivy & Ghosts Sitting On Rooftops

I inherit the fears of a child
Listening to the tumbling steps of a despotic father,
Alcohol-breathed, lecherous and rampant, up the stairs.

I inherit dreams that were killed as life burned itself out.

I inherit all the wounds that were covered up with silence.

The desecration of a girl. The infiltration. The bullying.
The body that she never got back.

The broken bones, the burning cigarette, threat-filled air,
    piss-stained,
Bones on the kitchen table, bones up my sleeve, winter
    windows,
Penetration, down my tongue, scratching the surfaces, *go
    play*,
Interiors, syringes, stinging, pestering, curdling underneath
    my skin.

I inherit non-consensual acts in marital beds.
I inherit the force of men onto women's bodies.
The resentment, the shivering, the smells, the out-of-body
    mechanisms.
Don't tell me that it is not real, it isn't mine, it isn't ours,
I
Feel

It
In
My
Bones.
The repercussions, the smile that hides disgust, docile, infuriated,
Get your hands off me, vicious circles, lullaby, pregnancy, not mine,
Not yours, there is no *ours, lay still, woman, lay still, girl, lay still and*
It will be over soon, two kinds of women, both subservient to men's desires,
And what about mine, what about ours, I've seen your face within me
And nothing disturbed me more.

The dead cling to the agency of our bodies.
Are you listening to your own body
Or the broken spirit of another?
A game lost or never played?

Tears, glass, frozen, gas, invisible, surrendering,
Everything swamps its way back in,
Into a body where everything gets stuck,
Where nothing is let out, where the unwanted stays
And degenerates and grows, and I must watch,
And I seem to cannot get my voice across,
A part of me, parts of me, staring and colliding.

All The Words You Left Behind

I write because you never heard a word I said
Because I never found my words
In front of your twitching face.

That gargantuan blasting hole
The exasperated jaw
The shrieking symphony of violence
Blood boiling under my skin
Tearing me apart
Inside out, outside in
Your voice losing its strings
The body unleashing its force
Onto me.

The body of a child.

Tongues in my ear
Breath on my cheeks
Saliva on my face.

Hands on me.
Hands on me.

In darkness
In my dreams
It was all just a dream
You have an imagination that is too vivid

For your own good.
I escaped.

I wanted to
Be safe
From you and
Your distorted and idealised sense of reality.

That you shoved my face in
My language in
My whole body in.

Oven fires.

Gasping
Touched, touched, touched amidst the flames
Cradling ashes, cradling flesh
You master of magic and resurrection
I tried to escape
Regain my strength
And you pulled and whispered

What have I done?

I invented words for my protection
For your protection.

What are you doing?
What are you doing?
What is your voice doing in my head?
What is your scent doing on my skin?
What is your language doing in my mouth?
Your thoughts in my flesh?

Dancing to your tune

Tripping over, falling over, losing balance.

And you will look at me.

(*So, I have failed you as a father?*)
(Reproach)
(How dare you?)

Freedom is something you took
You needed company to suck on
You needed company in your comfort zone ruins.
And you never wanted to get better,
Rise out of your misery,
You wanted me there.

A child choking on survival mechanisms.

A Body Within A Body Within A Body

The hands grow long
And it can never be simple
The touch from yesterday
Turning into the one from today
The scent attached to the skin
Besieging everything beneath the surface
Of you, of us, the names we carry,
The names that we wear like crowns
That try to hold on to us
Maybe captivate us, suffering co-dependently.

This is what we're like,
What we'll always be and succumb to,
Ourselves, the voices we've been given,
The thoughts we were thinking,
The destruction we cultivated
Of everything within us turned outward,
Turned inward once more,
Fumes of illegitimate poison,
Spreading its burning wings,
Onto the skies of night and dust and shells within clouds.

The alphabet of our bodies,
Steps tracing themselves back,
The taste of your lips
On the hard bed of our necks
Pecking, regurgitating, whispering

Thunder and tumultuous lies and cobwebs
Entailing you and your echoes
Spinning themselves into the fabric of our hair,
Our minds and hands, puppets hanging on by a thread,
A smile on your face, a smile so sad
And disastrous, it burns and disintegrates once it appears,
It asks and begs and kills for the fuel it needs.

Maintain me, hold me up, my lips,
My mouth, hold my heart and don't you dare break it,
Hold it, let it beat, be the heartbeat, if you let it fall
I'll smother you, I suffocate, I know death too well, its breath
Torments my spine, cradles my body, hands around my
    throat,
Am I am killer of selves, my own, is killing the right word,
Is that me, who am I within your body?

I died a long time ago and here I am, still talking to you,
Telling you what you should do, listen over here,
Follow my voice within you, am I right, why do you keep
    listening,
To me, I have lost my body, your voice barely knows
Its own sound, how to speak up, how to respond to me
And my vicious instructions or am I benevolent,
I don't know anymore, it's been such a long time,
I can't decipher my own impulses and actions anymore.

Dirty Fingernails

Can you hear it?
That's the sound.
The sound of my skin burning away,
Under your fingertips, ebbing away,
Knees melting onto the ground,
Spine laid bare, exhaling you.
Tobacco and aftershave,
Drool and grand gestures,
Here with me,
I pray with thunders in my mind,
To you, resurrect, don't die, live, everything
Intertwined, in and out, up and down,
One word becomes another.
And I dig for all the meanings
Trying to find my way out of the dirt
To breathe and understand
My hands full
Of the earth you left behind
That I'm trying to decipher and nurture
And love, always, no question, I'm slipping
Tripping, losing, hands full, hands on,
Your footsteps are gone, it's dark
And I try to breathe and bring you back up
Patching the roots back together
Life and death, resuscitate,
What?

You Tried To Take My Own Language Away From Me

I fled. I fled when I was bursting.
With a smile on my face.
Knives stuck in my body.
Nobody saw them.
Nobody saw me.

The ones who did, saw me
As a victim, as another chance,
As an endless opportunity to do harm,
To empower themselves and rid me of my name,
To do to me what they wanted to
Never caring that somebody had destroyed and twisted
My language, but you all find each other,
You all know each other, your games and patterns inside out,
You leave traces, condemned ones, wherever you go
So you know you can play, so they know my body
Is a playground, an elastic band that you can pull
And strain, exploit and masticate, yet is always coming
    back to itself,
Despite your inflictions and torments.

I lost nouns and verbs, they all meant another thing,
A body without a language, a language without a body,
Everything was cut off precisely, disconnected cleanly,
I agreed to things I did not comprehend,
To words that promised me treasures in old bottomless
    male anatomies

Where I'd get stuck looking for love and affection
And you'd take me, from all sides, absorb me, dry-mouthed.

And I still tried to look attractive
Even though I felt death within me.

Motionlessness, fear, concentrated and lingering,
The pressure to be still and docile and please,
To utter things against my own body
And call it *pleasure*, call it *lust*,
And I fled when I had the chance,
I always did, turn my back on you.

Body destructive,
(You became the dust you always had been)
Body poetic,
(Inner child)
I fled and closed all doors behind me.
There was a time when memories were my worst enemy.
I've stopped fighting them.
The point is that they weren't the end of the story.

The Archaeologist's Memory

You pretend that you cared about her.
You never got to know her.
And despite her obsession,
She knew in her bones
That parts of her needed to remain locked away
Because you hurt with a passion, you like the smell of
    blood,
You like girls on their knees,
You excel when you hear them scream
Their pain out of their hearts
And they sicken and can't get away from you
And your self-serving repetitive schemes.
You want to possess them, all, in fragments,
Buried and dug up, you bathe in their despair,
Your lungs get so full,
The perfume of disaster,
Your lips pressed onto competitive flesh,
They do everything wrong,
You make them feel so bad, so exhausted,
So attached to the unwholesomeness that is you,
To their inner lack, the call for help, the need for approval,
And you stuff their mouths, full,
And they overeat, undereat, can't spit you out,
You weave yourself into the texture of their skin
And intend to stay there forever, extracting their self-worth,
Stained, blood red, ghost white, off the street,
Thornbush, don't pretend, she knows this story well.

When The Girl Stopped Pleading

I looked at your hands
And thought, *I don't want my hands to end like that*,
I took hers in mine and felt so comforted,
So warm within the cold and robust,
We found each other there,
Held each other there, I spoke and she was silent,
She rose out of her own ashes to hold me
And she had a strength that I haven't seen since,
A sensitivity and empathy that I long for in everybody
    else,
I found in her beautiful old hands.

What happened to those hands that I loved,
Now that they belong to you in death,
Now that you are within the crowns of trees,
Effortlessly, breathing in and out,
Wandering through the colours of leaves,
The touch of your hands lingers on my skin
And everything beneath, the texture of our love
And affection, you never left me alone.

You were always there until you weren't.

And his hands that I rage against
Pull me towards his mouth
And all I want to do is screech
Into his merciless face.

I didn't want to have
Violent hands.
I taught myself that I had to fight
If I wanted to survive.
He wanted me to fall apart,
Take one hit after another and pretend that nothing happened
That we were healthy the way we were, the way we acted.

It took years to get out of my head.

I wired myself against him and yet
I could fall back from womanhood into childhood instantaneously.

The Birth Of Venus

I hear the language of the dead in my body.

In my head, their hands lost their matter,
The texture of their fox-trotting thoughts
Seek electrification through mine,
Through interaction, through connection,
And I used to crop them, deracinate them like
Pest weeds, but my voice contains affected roots.
I embody ancestral cacophonies.

I looked at you and thought about ways to escape you.
I didn't know that you lived in my body as well.

I listened to your screams and cries and gave you life
Whilst planning my resignation, my coming-of-age
In my childhood, running far away from you,
The things you jolted in my head, in my body,
I wanted to shed the calluses of your skin,
I wanted to rid myself of you and your language
That messed with my own.

You begged for love and acceptance and compassion
At my door (I put all my powers in my key)
And I shut you out, the wailing, the apologies
Too well-known, too premeditated, too well-formed,
You abused them, dried them out, your hands on my head,
A curse on my scalp, your words in my ear,

And I thought, *I have to get out of here.*

I left you behind. I tried.
I failed in layers and succeeded in layers.
I approached you, us, from very different angles
And discovered you in my everyday steps,
In moments caught off-guard,
In my expression, my breaths, my gestures,
There, you, us, do I exist at all,
Or am I a reproduction, of you, of them all,
Tracing themselves back into existence, into life?

Who is the leech, who is sucking blood,
Who draws my body in, who fights in whose arena,
(Why are we fighting at all?)
Am I a construct, contaminated, boisterous with your
    moods
That ceased to die when fires tore bones apart,
And I, with all my forces, made my way into this world
And you thought you could try anew
And I fought and fought, blindly, claiming that
I am my own creation.

The Ingestion Of Terror

I carry the death of us in my bones.

The tenses underneath my skin.
The names I gave myself, the ones you gave me.
The way you looked at my body,
The way you touched my body.

I wasn't holding it. I was out of control,
And yet my hands got caught in a spider's web,
Moving around, entwined, misguided, infested,
Rotating, your warmth promising shelter,
Promising a home, I could only feel bones,
Bodies without a heart, bodies without a pulse
And you grabbed me, closer, tighter, stamping
Yourself onto me, tracing yourself back to me,
Saying *this is mine, this belongs to me*,
It weaves itself around, me, unaware, ever-wanting,
Self-inflicted, sense of self, torn, life and death,
Endless submission, of myself, itself, our selves, the way you
    talk,
I should have listened.

Your intentions were in your fingertips,
And you scratched and punched, your smile, clandestine,
The rotten ensnarement, nothingness, destruction, in your veins
That preach love with a mask on, hard-on, hand to hand,
    second-hand,

Dry throat, empty heart, pulling bodies towards yours with toxic glue,
You want the world to burn because it hurts.

Ending regeneration, ending upon the tongues of women that are girls,
Lust that rips their hearts out, *eat it, eat it, suck it,*
And they're swallowing you, *body miserable, body misogynistic,*
And they deaden inside, you get aroused as you watch them burn,
Melt in your hands, tethered into your flesh,
You suck, blood and tears, heartbeats, you shred and discard
And tell them to come back, tethered, into your fabric and skills,
Your passion kills, exhausts, disappoints.

Vicious cycle after vicious cycle, the choirs of women losing their voices,
And you plunged into their bodies, the collector's vice,
And you try to survive with a woman's will to thrive.

The Light In My Bones

In retrospect, it gives me joy to remember you
Standing in your garden, amongst the roses and mint
 leaves,
Amongst self-erected trees and compost heaps,
Right beneath the sun, the way you wore your fisherman's
 hat,
And walked through all the colours with a sense of pride
And achievement, your dreams instilled in this garden
And I would forget all the empty promises.

Time was running out, energy was running out,
The dead life taking hold of you,
And I start to make my peace with you now,
All the things that never came out, all the things that
Have always remained unsaid, always floating mutely
In choking waves of air, entwined, within my own body,
The language of us, your body and mine, theirs and ours,
Ours, all of us, trying to become separate entities,
Trying to wrestle and detach ourselves, rename ourselves,
Establish different circumstances and shift and carve out
 new roots.

(We have never been wildflowers)

And *you*, of course, the end came slowly, you thought
 about it
All the time, the end, the ending, from within, projected

Into the outside, you gave so much, and you grew old,
And you'd think with sass, *just come get me already*,
I've lived enough.
I feel your peace now, your freedom, now,
I love to remember your scent, fresh, powdery, classy,
The way you sat amongst people, eating your ice cream,
As if you were a child still, as if you could finally enjoy it,
Pay for it, sitting there, watching people move and pass
    you by,
And you'd sit there, for hours, thinking your thoughts,
Remembering them for us, your jokes and light-hearted
    judgements.

You made me laugh, *coming home*, the way you dressed,
    your hair, you
Took care of yourself, most of the time, the generosity,
    details that made you
Unforgettable, I put your scent on my own skin,
And you live in me still, and I hold you there and keep you
    so warm.

I've always loved you, your eloquence and vulgarity alike,
Your fierceness and fearfulness, your care and chaos,
All the things that you never revealed but stayed with you,
All the things that you expressed by not saying them
And took with you, you loved with your body,
You loved with your presence, your actions and gestures,
And I filled in the blanks with words.

Will You Make Yourself Sick?

You carry the dead within you,
Those who came before you
Those who helped create you, mould you,
Innumerable pairs of hands, minds and bodies
And they persist as you persist
You can love them, you can reject them
Everything grows, you decide what grows within you and
　　how.

Are you going to make yourself sick
Or are you going to heal?

Are you going to make things better,
Heal the dead, love the dead no matter what,
Cure ancestral dreams and longings
As you feel them inside of you in your own voice,
A tree that needs to grow and reach undiscovered heights,
Not a fire that threatens to spread?

What will they tell you if they see you retreat?
Will they sieve through your skin, their vices and virtues?
Put patterns in your language, tones in your mouth?
Images in your head? Are they coming back to you?
Do they come to you because you're the one in need?
And you swallowed them already, by having been born,
And you ask yourself who you are in contrast to them.
You want to be different, become someone else,

And yet you're scared of the unknown,
You are the unknown.

Who are you in communication with them?

You don't want to repeat the old that failed in your eyes,
You want to rethink, recreate yourself and you cut yourself off.
Who are you then, amongst the multitude of people?

Who do you belong to, where did you come from,
What do you feel, what remains, what's your name?
What does it mean to be you amongst the many,
Amongst the past that is you, that isn't you,
What do you mean, you, who will follow you,
And what will they say, will you end up in a shadow,
Or in the limelight, distorted by controversy, disagreement,
Or will you be taken care of?
Did you make it into a value system of future generations?
Did you make it better? Were you better?

What do the memories and stories of you
Feel like in my body, in my bones, in my heart
And what can I do about them? What will I do with them?

Turn my back on you and myself, parts thereof,
Or will I take a good look at you and myself and
Give us both a hand to end this loneliness, the
Excommunication, this blocked state of existence
Sickening itself in effortless regretfulness and mournful silence.

The Language Of Memorabilia

At some point you need to say *yes* to the past.
Yes, that's its face, that's its language, that's its behaviour.

We made it together, an irreconcilable thing of beauty and
    ugliness,
Always in transformation, in regression, digression,
Growing multiple heads, twisted in too many directions,
We were always armed with negligence and a lack of
    intimacy,
A desire to move, forwards, away, in resentment and
    frustration.

Looking at faces, thinking about the possibility of love
Touching bodies rejecting dreams that were not ours
That tasted wrong on our tongues, cold on our skin
Hot on theirs, hot in their minds,
And we ran so far away, in our gown of shadows and
    chains,
Trying to shed what had not been ripe yet,
Having seen where it would go, where it would all go
    wrong
And we couldn't escape, we would be hurt,
We were made to revolt and close our eyes and think of
    better days
Not look into the eyes of those who inflict pain
Not focus on our own hands that dragged memorabilia
Through the mud that people would never find again

When they grow old and nostalgic
Looking for hideous dissolved and aching rays of light
And refine the goodness, that minuscule particle
That might have given them hope
When life could still be saved.

The Butcher Of Intuition

What would have happened
If you hadn't burned down
The soil that you raged and rested on?

Would it have been easier for me to move?
Would I have felt my own body?
Wouldn't your words have overwritten my own texture?

Overruled my gestures, would I have existed
And lived outside of your dictation?

I was a cloud when I should have been the tempest.
I cried when I should have yelled.
I smiled when I despaired.
You tore out one brick after the other
And told me that I should be a fortress
Whilst your hands ruined me
And I was forced to find shelter amongst the bricks you stole.

Parts of my strength crawling into you, aggrandised and reinforced,
Integrated, your own exploitative fortress,
And I lost faith in the holiness of my abandoned and revisited ruins
As I trusted ancestral hands instead of my own body.

Dialogues Passing By

Making my peace with you is the most deep-seated battle.
You've become the face of death and I wonder
What is going on inside your head now,
Are you still the same in there?

It makes me sick to my stomach to see you.
I'm composing myself. I'm still a child in your eyes.
Your expression still tries to bully me into self-sacrifice.
And I still see women form the holy trinity around you.
You feel heavy in my gut.
And in a split second, I'm back in your madhouse,
With fire in my throat that burns my insides
Whilst I forbid myself to speak
Because you pretend that we live in an alternative reality
And I don't know how to talk to you
Because I see the terror of your face when met with contradictions.

I question whether the amount of guilt and shame I sense
Fully belongs to me.
Did I accept it as part of myself when I had no idea
What that actually meant?
I took responsibility before I even learned the word.

I've stopped punishing myself.
(The more I apologised the bloodthirstier people got)

I acted out of the mess you left within me.
The older I got the more I felt like a child.
And I started to realise that the way I was acting
Was an unreflected imitation of your behaviour that
I had internalised as my own impulses over the years
And that had nothing to do with who I was.
And I accepted all the things that I had done wrong
When I wasn't myself
When I thought I was myself
When you told me who I was
When you told me who I could never be
When I was crumbling under your roof.
You taught me how to be a feather
So that you could be the wind.

Autumnal Introspections | Inner Child

I heard you scream and revolt
Right underneath my skin
Where your voice faltered
Crashing against my edges and roundabouts
You'd listen to my internal promises
And the following self-disappointment,
The deceit that had no definition yet,
Trying to make the body crumble into action,
Into understanding, into feeling you.

You asked me questions through my throat,
You barely made it onto my tongue
You were too brave, too straightforward,
Knew what you wanted, always, but
I faced the outside world and let it outweigh you,
Outpour you, flood you, smashed against my organs
That agreed with you and tried to echo your voice
Upwards, inside out, it was always time to listen.

You fought so hard within my body for love,
And when I hit rock bottom inwardly
You sighed and held me tightly and
We rustled warmly, autumnal leaves,
And shone in unison and serenity.

Nuances

I was created, hands added their texture,
Hands moulded mine, words dove straight
Into my self-deprecating vocabulary, echoes that were not
　　mine,
Voices, forlorn, ever-expanding, across my unborn
Skin, layer after layer, they sang to me, sang
Me to life, held me there, stewing, stretched
To the left, pulled to the right, squeezing
Into myself to stay close to my own heart.

Nowhere to hide, nowhere to resign,
I heard them, enter and develop,
Shades into my ears, a concoction of the past
A promise for the future, survival, I wonder whose,
From theirs, to hers, to mine, poking my body
With fingernails and stomachaches, holding
On to lives that are lived and gone, holding
On to a body unborn, mine, with their heartaches and chaos,
Their ambiguities and indecisiveness, neediness,
Everything they hadn't done.

They speak to my body and I cannot be alone
From the beginning, I have never been alone,
I am part of a choir that is etched into my flesh,
They all scream at me, wanting more and more,
Taking over, the dead invaded me within the womb
And as I was born, they were reborn too.

From A To Z And Nothing In-between

I tried to make my peace with you and
Your actions prematurely.

I tried to focus on everything that went on
Beneath the rage, the outbursts, the violence
In the air that I inhaled, mouth to mouth,
Gut to gut, but it came at a price.

I saw how broken you were inside and why,
And you realised my understanding and abused it,
Played with it, you were fire and I was ash, lived on my
	compassion,
In your hands, draining me, your mouth kept
Raging and punching, your mind kept defeating everyone
	in its path,
Invisibly, slowly, poisoned compliments, a smile on your
	threatening face,
I provided you with all of my empathy, I trusted your pain,
	and
Let you in, and you twisted everything inside,
Tearing me apart, exhausting your welcome.

I tried to find peace, a cure for your behaviour against me,
Against my figure, everything that looked like you.
You never let go of your infectious self-loathing.

I let you feed me with it.

I tried to find a drop of goodness in it until my heart went numb.
Something worthwhile within you that I could nurture into creation.
You exasperated the bodies of women
And didn't stop at the body of your mother.
Everything started there.

The body of your sister,
Sickness to sickness.
The body of your wife,
Doing what you wanted.
In the name of love (what you called *it*)
(what is *it*?)

The body of your daughter(s),
Lines are drawn, slowly, there to stay,
Lines of femininity, erased boundaries.
I concentrated so much on the causes of the fire
That I missed my inner deaths because I swallowed your smoke.

Rope & Leash

I fell from your cold arms
Right into the ashes that
Escaped your sleeves.

Right into the valley of your legs,
And I tried to define love then
And there.

I lost everything except for
The air in my crouched body,
I sought language and looked at your
Mouth, waiting for a sound, for
A benevolent word, a word that resonated with me,
To raise expectations, that I could
Call mine, amidst these ashes that
Were now mine, your scent still on
My skin.

You handed me a rope and a leash,
They felt the same to me, time being
Exasperated, killed, slowly or abruptly,
You squeezed me tightly, and I started
Wondering, *what am I doing here*, you
Wanted yourself repeated, endlessly,
Echoed and copied, against the rhythm
Of my own heartbeat, you didn't care.
You wanted me to listen and internalise you,

Eternalise you, drown myself in my own skin,
Cold like yours, the warm ancestry of the world,
Beating, drumming, within our bodies,
Holding on to our vocal cords, pulling,
Dissatisfied, death came too early, unwilling
To give up their power amongst the living.

Force-fed

What happened to all the voices
That found life in the past and
Rose into the present, live within
Bodies, travelling from one to the
Next, holding on, persisting, without
A name and date, without matter, a mere
Purpose to do what, to repeat, to reconfigure
Vicious circles, make them more obvious,
More intense, more invincible, what has been
Suppressed and ignored, resisted and swallowed
In shame and embarrassment?

Have those voices been killed off?
Is that what light demanded collectively,
Rage against shadows, twist one another's arm
In a never-ending battle in black and white tones?
Why, what good will it do?
How could this ever help?

To Know What Rings True

There are days, maybe like today,
That make me want to scream at the
Whole world.

I am enraged. I am heartbroken.
I am fed up with the way things (don't) work
And bored to see how people lie to themselves.
Asking, *how are you*, and not waiting for an answer.
I'm good.
I'm good.
I'm good.

My smile serves you well.
The truth would be a thing misplaced.
Inappropriate.
You're buying a picture perfect illusion.
That's what you expect.
That's not what I am. That's not how I am.
Don't you dare believe it.

I can barely stand and hold it together and smile
At you to make you feel comfortable and welcome.

Why go back to a sense of normal that slowly killed us all,
Why party, party, party, drink and overeat to keep us numb,
Money out of our pockets, life out in the open, forced to
    work to afford living,

Down the glass, up the roof, through the drunken night sky,
Blind to ourselves, fighting and not caring, this rage
Banging its head against the wall, thinking it goes unseen,
Thinking it's obsolete, useless, nothing ever changes, the old
Song of lethargy that is never true, wake up, why don't you wake up?

You do and it hurts, they call it self-inflicted, it's the world we
Build with our cold hearts every single day, it doesn't feel
Like home, we shatter it all,
Pretending that we're having fun, never going deeper,
Empty words, empty gestures, *a little bit of hard-earned money*
And then you may have earned the right to live.
(It goes on and on)
(You've never signed that contract)
(And you can't get out of it)
(Because you want to live)

The bait tingling above our throats, unloved, neglected,
Why not dive straight into our own substantiality?

They made you believe that you consist of superficialities,
That being attached to the shallowness and deceitfulness of the dreams they told
Us we should have was attractive and in our best interest.
They used our virtues to feed their vices.

And you kept dancing to their tune that kept you down,
Kept drowning in their leftover lifestyle intended for you,
Don't let them make you sick, don't make yourself sick.

Don't be a martyr to a cause that is none
(Jobploitation)
And you don't
Even believe in, that dehumanises you and only pretends
  that you matter.
(*If you want to live you have to work*)
(I am alive, is that not reason enough to be able to live?)

Moths Amidst Fireworks

My voice sounds differently in my mind.
My inner voice has lots of vocal cords.
Every vocal cord makes me feel differently.
They are connected to the past.
They sound like the dead if I want them to.
I can barely remember my childhood voice.

I haunt myself. I keep myself company.
I talk aloud to the ones I've lost and they come back to me.
I can bring anything to fruition in my mind.

You wanted me to sound wrong and not like myself.
I don't want a voice that doesn't belong to me.
I don't want to strain my voice to sound better to you.
Accommodating, amenable, gullible, like a good little girl
In a woman's body. My inner child belongs to me, not you.
I am not here to please you with artificialities.

I don't want to sound happy when I'm not.

I liberate my voice from your expectations.

I still hear *you* say my name and I am home.

Burn The House Down

Have you ever been *a good girl?*
Have you felt guilty, repentant?
Hands running over my mouth,
Fingers through my hair, curse words,
From one ear to the next, the ringing
Sounds in my stomach, the heat, captured,
Resilient, persistent, up and down the whole
Body, within your grasp, stinging toxicity.
The fingers move around me like ropes,
Lace, enlarged, accumulated, thick, hair
Caught within the fabric, the textures of
Your bitterness and emptiness,
Your shattered dreams that you never dreamed of,
Considered, evaluated, tossed to the side, of the road,
Crushed, without stopping, hit-and-run, blood on
Your scalp, painted my body with that blood,
With that frustration and disappointment,
The sick hope and envy you injected my skin with.
You and I, we moved violently towards and away
From each other, I had your face and turned it into
My own, I walked through the scaffold you erected
For me and burned it to the ground, I came out alive
And feel my own name resonate in my strong bones,
Across every single organ, I holler and rage and love
And set myself free on a daily basis, you made the universe
Your nemesis, I create myself anew and incorporate it in
   every part of my own body.

Pantomime

What happened in the overt cracks?
The cracks forced and shoved back together,
Disappearing amongst the weight of one another,
Disinformed, overwhelmed, stifled, hunted, chipped,
A piece at a time, traversing, flooded, overrun by old
Patterns, blemished and targeted, pressured into a corner
To conform, to crouch and beg, the raped generations,
The ancestral sins, the running blood, the dead water,
The benediction of decay, hands on me, hands on you,
Face to face, so blind, so silent, take me away, I'm made
Out of clay, my own, theirs, the ones who cannot rest, who
Still beg for forgiveness, what happened to us, what do
Our voices sound like, without theirs, a concoction of
  despair,
It's going to end, they are going to run out, how do I
  forgive,
How do I not resent,
I want to live,
I want to live,
I want to live,
Has there ever been protection, what did it consist of,
Where is the heart of the machine?
How can I reach the heart of the machine?

Daughterprey

deeply within
I never questioned
your reasons for
tormenting me
because you taught me that I
myself was the reason
because I was
because I am
*
you observed my face
and thought *no*
*
our home
was your backstage area
where all the masks fell off
and nobody would ever believe what we saw
*
when you were begging at my door
for forgiveness
whilst you were still posing a threat
I'd have done anything to make you disappear
*
from you
I learned that
my body was robbed of its boundaries
*
figlia di papà,

figlia di papà,
figlia di papà,
you make me sick

*

you created us
to destroy yourself

*

you made sure that
your grave
was big enough for all of us

Genii locorum

I wonder whether those silent walls are still charged
With the escapades of your shattering voice.
The violence within the bonework, across the
Skin, the hair, the smoke, the repulsive air, the
Scent of explosion, temper and falling onto the
Ground, shell across shell, windows bursting, bodies
Running, away, away from you, the things that
Jumped out of your mouth in a devastating hurry.

Are you still there? Is that where your voice stayed?
Is that where it went? The halls of reverberation.
The furniture destroyed and trashed. The animals
Feeling your rage, hiding, seeking your love, just like us.
Beggars, all of us, distorted, amputated, disconnected from
    you
And your merciless conscience that I never thought existed.

The place where I slept, accompanied by every single
Heartache, the wounds that never ceased to end, the
Windows reflecting my grimaces, my hopelessness,
The solitude, and the house got emptier and emptier,
Cleaner and desolate, the history seemed erased, it's all
In those walls, the desperation, the scrutiny, the dreams,
Out of the chimney, I know you're still there, as he is still
There, you're in certain rooms, in certain objects, out
Of my body, it had been way too long, I made a choice, I
    let you

Go, violently, perhaps, that was the language you spoke.
My dreams bring me back to my room, to hospital beds,
Basements, wine cellars, the houses I grew up in,
The façade and downfall of them all, how *she* ended up
All alone, in the midst of everything abandoned and gone,
And she refused to be as dead inside as the homes she
    stood in
And was still pressured to leave behind.

I saved myself, it was an act of love towards myself and
The life that I wanted to live outside of the walls you built
And which pretended that everything was so very well.

Mea culpā, mea culpā, mea máxima culpā

You pretended that you never knew what I
Was talking about.
We were never able to make it onto the same page
When we spoke to each other.
I knew where I stood when you let your body speak for itself.
You couldn't control your body,
Not the way you were in charge of your words.
You sent the past, that you steered me into,
Straight through the chimney, reformed the ashes,
And tried to send clouds into my brain, too,
But I always remembered you, the heavyweight traces you left behind.

What made you think that I would forget the nights when
Your screams woke me up and I was convinced that the world was burning.
I thought your throat was bursting as I heard our names in your mouth,
The way you destroyed our names in-between your jaw
Sank straight into my body like an anchor so that I would drown,
So that you could wash your hands clean.
(*You did this to yourself*)
This was you in my gut, this was you in my mind,
This was you in my face, my tears, my throat.
What is it now? You exploded like clockwork.

Stop screaming. Stop screaming.
(*I'm calling the police. I called* you.)

You're so scared and unwilling to recall what I recall,
To admit it all, to claim responsibility for once,
Shed a light on the demons that you exposed to us so vividly,
In merciless harassment, a daily routine, straight
Into the abyss, that I grew up in, that I scratched my
Way out of with my will to live still intact.

How can you still pretend and envelop
Yourself in sweet tones and colours,
And not smell the blood on your hands?

The Spectacle Of Disintegration

I stood alone in that big house where everything happened,
To say goodbye.
The house that contained all of our stories,
Our lives and deaths.
Our childhood faces and fears, secrecies and dreams.
I took as much as I could with me,
The little pieces of beauty that gave me hope.
The rooms destroyed, dissected and deserted.
It was built as a dream that wasn't meant to end,
Only to fall apart from within.
You created a paradise with the instruments
Of hell, it wouldn't work, it would disintegrate,
Hurt itself, hand in hand, a torrent of self-destruction,
One household imitated another,
Extracting and exacerbating the worst,
Neighbours peeking through their foul-faced curtains.

I stood in that echoing space, I couldn't
Turn the light off, death never stopped knocking
On the doors, the windows looking into me
And I stood there, waiting for people to come back,
To come home, to reappear, as if no time had passed,
As if the present were a liar, standing in a nightmare that
    finds its end
In the present moment, what was still going on within me,
Torn between two households, touch evaporated once it
    reached my fingertips,

The floor that our bodies landed on, the windows that our bodies were
Thrown out of, how we ran away, from one home to another,
The walls incarcerating all the screams from yesterday.

I find you here, still, with me, the moving perpetrator,
You made me turn to darkness for comfort, you made me
Speak to the dead, the lesser evil, I had more hope in the dead,
The ones that couldn't touch me anymore, tell me to fetch things,
Be a good girl, the empty kitchen table, objects obsolete,
The past mourning the present.
Everything dust and dead matter, everybody gone, under the night
Sky, away from your walls, the walls that hid the wars that went on,
The walls that pretended that everything was all right,
Just like every other house,
The walls, these murdering edges that you erected around your monstrosity.

Die unersättliche Gier der Drangsale: Tribulations Of Insatiable Greed

You entered my body through my stomach,
The sound of your voice, bursting, rummaging,
I tried to shoot it out of my ears, but there you
Lingered, on the wrong side of the eardrum,
Banging, accepting the bad things into my ear,
The lies, the factory of heartbreak, the deconstructive
Criticisms, the regurgitating saboteurs, you selected
What was allowed to make its way in and I lost control,
I didn't know that what I had to fight was wearing so many
    masks.

You caused disruption within me.
Every reaction forecast, out of character, mine.
You drenched my body to replicate yourself
(*I let myself be taken*)
And beat yourself up, out of your body,
Away with yours, through mine, this vision of yours,
Sick (taking what you need) your ejections, rejections,
    projected
On my skin to shred to pieces.

You blinded me and I did not see who I was anymore.
You needed me to be a blank page so you could have all the
    words.
I observed everything that came out of your mouth wide open,

(When she dared to look into your eyes when you were
   taking what you needed, she stared into two dead black
   pupils)
And I learned my lessons by heart, knowing that you
Would never stop until you gained the last piece of me,
I learned to open my mouth too and instead of taking
You in, absorbing you, I chose to bare my teeth and bite
   and grind hard
Until you would stop coming close to me.

Daughterperspective

You didn't need your body anymore
To continue the damage that you
Initiated, you made sure that you'd
Survive through the stories they'd repeat.

Your life's work through hyperboles,
Cheating your way into a sense of peace.
You use women's mouths to remain impactful.
Rid yourself of guilt, abuse your own sickness.
You want to be held in high regards and wipe out our
    memories.

You rely on us to find the impossible love within us,
The one that you never even tried to find.
I don't feign forgiveness.

I can sense her over my shoulder when I write.
Too much she took to her grave, she's bursting still,
Aching to find relief, find the words, the truth that nobody
    would have believed.
Her arms still reach out, so far, I feel
Them on my skin, the broken heart in my chest,
The unchallenged strength that someone dared to
    decompose.

Healing Just One Part At Least

Men appear by my side, they feel like
You, the little things I liked about you,
On your good days, the way you used to dress,
The way you smelled when you left home, your glasses, the way
You combed your hair, maybe there is a
Way back to love, without the sound, without
Letting you in on your worst days, keeping these
Little holy things that promised me something to see the light
That you suffocated within you.

These men appear and sometimes I pretend
That I didn't see them, that the thought of you
Didn't cross my mind, that I don't know that you're
There, in that horrible room, and I'm here, safe from
What you cannot be anymore, and yet, it had always
Been your mind, you see, the body I could handle,
But it was the mind, the voice, the whole act that
Almost crushed me, I would never go back to that.

And yet these men appear and I don't know what to do,
Somehow, exactly, I look at their shoes, what they purchase,
And they take me to you, maybe in the safest way possible,
A route where love can just be without intimacy, without
Speech and touch. I take you there. Not the other way around.
We meet each other like this, through these

Unknown men who disappear after an instant,
Who reveal to me a love amputated from all the
Hardships and in this realm it can live, it may live, and
   maybe you
Feel it too, and they reappear in the middle of a city.

Totenstille / Deathly Quiet

I was locked into a room with you
And your insanity. I wondered how
Long it would take to absorb it as well.

I asked myself, would it enter my body
At all? Does the confined space make me
Less resilient, more impressionable?

What would decide my defeat?
Your victory against me? Would it be the time
Spent with you in darkness? Or the corseted space?

Or would it be me, my ears, my eyes, my mind
Open, my wounds letting you in, letting you
Heal my wounds instead of doing it myself?

Or would you make it physical, the dance, to crawl
Under my skin?

Auseinandersetzung / Altercation

Your words came a long way.
I think I gave them legs, I may
Have given them mine.

By mistake. I didn't fully understand
What I had done. I just wanted to
Help you. Help you out of your
Misery. Enable you to take new steps.
Towards life.

I incorporated your words.
I gave them more life through movement,
I ran away from them without knowing
That they had long lived stitched to my
Own vocal cords.

Your voices were fighting with mine
In my head and I thought that's all me,
I am chaotic, I am destructive, I am falling
Apart. I scratch my skin until it bleeds, I have
Seen it elsewhere, I've seen *her* doing that, and
Her voices and the ones infiltrating her, the texture
Had been sewn, the faces mingled, skin within skin,
She had been done, for her it was too late, I've seen her
Die, in my mind, I've felt her there, fighting and losing
All battles and wars, I couldn't allow your words
To tear down my white flags that I hold so close to my body.

Your voices needed life, to exist, to contaminate, to possess
And rob, you wanted me left with nothing, except endless
Apologies to you, endless fake gratitude, endless clinging to
You, blinded and silly, you never wanted me to grow up, taking
The credit for everything good, that I made work, after all, my
Victories you construed as yours, wanting me to be dependent on
You, thinking it's all you, it could never be me,
And my legs never felt like my own.

I allowed you to disconnect me from my own body.
To start the swallowing process from my feet upwards.
Abusing my hands, my mind, chasing the wrong people,
To feel the heel on my neck, again and again, you taking over,
One gutted life story after another, circles of shards, cracked mirrors.

Your words led to actions.
Your actions became mine.
Your mental illness set root and rot within my body.

But something within me had always put up a good fight

That never seemed to end, that would never give up,
Never bow to the injustices done, always stepping up,
I let my own voices sing in choirs, Father,

I raised myself as a loud daughter.

Louder than you, louder than the words
You shoved down my throat, I have always been more than
Ready to revolt and uproot what's grown too comfortable
In my skin that has never been yours to begin with.

Internalising The Body Language Of Ghosts

You never responded to the result
Of your actions, the terrible end product
That would never end, that always set ends
To everybody and everything in slow motion,
In taught motion, yours, everlasting, ever-burdening,
Her shoulders, moulded by your condemnations,
The pitfall of your nails, the flesh, her salty skin
On the bed, on the tip of your tongue, stardust, erased,
Forgotten, swallowed, in a haze.

(*Forget what happened here / She hates herself for it*)

Your mother told you how awful women were,
How despicable, how stupid, she fought against her
Own sex, disconnected from herself and her body,
The men that beat her put on a pedestal, a man's right,
She let destruction happen to her, teaching her boys
That women are the worst and she would take their punches,
Orchestrating her own demise, why, and for what, they'd
See her as the only exception, maybe that was the point,
The holy mother, the only good woman amongst them all.

But she hated herself. She didn't live, she gave, her life,
To you, you devoured it, took every piece of her flesh,
She considered it rubbish, disembowelled, away with it,
Into the mouths of men, away from her, *mother*
    misogynistic,

The sex, unfelt and gone, the breasts in the way, untouched,
    unappreciated, dead meat,
She banished them from her body, out of mind, flesh
    bursting
From her flesh, nothing more, she dehumanised herself
For the sake of raising boys, she broke them, they
    internalised her discarded
Sense of self, misinterpreting it as love,
Her depreciation of everything female, so repulsed.

And she had a daughter. *The weak duplication.* The body of
    pure agony.
The sufferer. All of them. I wonder how she must have felt
    under
Your mother's damaged touch, the father's incessant violence,
Showing it off, the vicious power, the abuse, his hands, his
    fits,
How he was still the king of his own world, everybody
    crouching
And shivering, wanting to be hurt, wanting to feel connected,
Feel their bodies through pain, it's what they could get
From them, all they could get, the comfort of the familiar, the
Prison, still idealised, still praised, still replicated.

There's a reason why you were the way you were
But you stayed that way on purpose.
There's a reason why she is mentally ill.
Stuck in a marriage, taking the beatings.
Letting her son be shunned, nowhere to be found.
The code of honour is to never break the vicious cycles.

Every generation owning it to the other to stick to the
    inherited guns.
Loyal to the blood-stained dead.
And wade through the same old dysfunctions.

All of you, planting insane seeds, keeping it going.
The mother, beaten to death.
The brother wandering aimlessly from one mental
   institution to the next,
Almost eviscerating his own family with his urge for
   decomposition.
The daughter calls herself a lost cause too, addicted to the
   suffering,
Thinking she couldn't do it as well and gracefully as her
   mother,
Couldn't live up to the mothersaint, accepting the sickness
   to spread.
She is doing the same thing to her daughter, devouring
   her,
Needing her until death parts them both.

And then there's you.

You, the other brother, you thought you were better,
You who fled, but took it all with you
Anyhow just to end up creating your own version of it,
Thinking you're liberated without ever realising that every
Single part of you was still living in that warzone that
   never
Wanted to end, until almost all of us, shut you out, cut it
   out, stopped it,
Then and there, here and now, every single day.

Urteilsvermögen / Discernment

I wonder when it all went wrong.
Did it already happen within her, that
Nothing was right from the start?
When he put his hands on her, when
He told her that she wanted it, when
He persuaded her to let him in, once more,
Had it not been decided yet that things had
Already fallen apart and the last pieces would
Be sliced off?

He took her, made you, they did, and everything
Started to unravel, he wanted to pin her onto him,
He wanted her to stay and linger and dissolve further,
He thought you could make sure of that, that she stays,
That she cannot leave, that your presence would change her
Mind, that it would assure her dependency.

You used your children. You made her so that she would save you.
You always used them to get what you wanted, to keep her with you,
No matter how much hurt you made them swallow.

It never worked, did it? You put such a burden on her
That she'll never comprehend. You created duplication
After duplication of *her*, never gone from your mind and

Yet all the cheating, all the excess, the begging for sex, the
Erasure of women's identities, laughable, all of them, in
   your
Hands, in your train of thought, you couldn't get enough, you
Needed to remain in power, you were always the one who
   leaves,
She couldn't do that to you, take your move away from
   you, the
Taste of your own medicine, and what about that little girl
   on
Whose shoulders you put the weight of your world turned
   upside-down?
She came to this world and was so fragile and you'd never
Touch her, but you invaded her in so many invisible ways,
   the
Favourite, so it seemed, that never mattered, you always
   had
A plan, it always ran parallel with destruction sold as love
   and
Affection, she was meant to repair the state of things that
   could
Never step back into the past, how it was, how broken it
   had always been,
She was meant to keep her there, in your prison, to make
   her
Visualise the harm she'd inflict, but careful there, it was
   you who
Made it impossible to stay, you broke it all, you started the
   fire.
You always mastered the art of reassigning blame.
And you moulded her in your image. Your character
Beneath her looks. The older she got, the more she
Started to look like you. And then you couldn't handle her
Anymore, when you came out in her, when you erupted
   within her,

What you did, to her, how you were, everything you hated,
Within her, inside out, the conflictual nervous-compulsive nature,
The soul-gutting narcissism, the intrigues, the lies, the whole act,
The tragedy swallowed by everyone, the inner perpetrator burning
Within their own skin. That's on you. She's on you.
You never faced your demons.
And you encouraged her to become one of them.
And now you are not facing her either, letting her fall, too,
Because you never loved yourself and you never loved
Her either. And it shows.

Using A Little Girl As A Pawn To Win A Game That Is None

The first thing that she learned
From you was powerlessness, a lie.
You invaded her new-born body and made her feel
Responsible for saving your marriage.
You were in need of love, intimacy and affection
And took them from a girl who trusted her father,
The transgressions, the dark sides of love,
That the women you surrounded yourself with
Couldn't convey and started to decline.

Nothing else mattered. You held her and
She didn't question the way you seemed to love her.
Your body against hers. Trusted you to know what
Love is, make her feel what you felt.

You pretended. You made her believe in an idyll.
You used her to project it. All you wanted is to
Keep your prison going. Planted her there as the
Only factor to consider, a vessel, an object, *you can't
Leave, you can't leave me now, can you? You'd be the monster,
You'd be heartless*, and you played the victim with a doubt-
    erasing talent.

She was a little child. She couldn't repair what you destroyed.
She should never have become your pawn. That was never

on her.
You wanting her to fix things with her presence, never
 yourself.
Do you have any idea what you have done?
Of course it would fail. She'd never understand
What was wrong with her.
You.
You were wrong.
Burdening her with the impossible.
Blaming her. Abandoning her when she became useless
To you, when she started to grow and revolt and reveal the
 same face as yours.

Ausgangspunkt / Point Of Origin

It was one of your worst nights.
You couldn't see things clearly.
And yet, something had touched you,
Something resonated, the bells rang,
Right across your ears, you felt the truth
Of your body in your body, the bonework,
The blood work, infiltrated, the heart,
Never light as a feather, and you could hear the
Truth, and it hurt as it stepped in, into your mind,
Drastically.

The little girl that lived in sorrow and silence,
Stepping up, stepping forwards, revelatory,
She showed you, she told you, *this is what happened*,
To you, to me, to us, these images are ours, within us,
Here I am, this is my voice, the forlorn dialogues,
The suffocated words, the language erased from my body,
Take me now, take it in, again, look at it now, *look at my
    hands*, feel them again,
My feet, the belly, the head, how they talked to us, into it,
Their way into us, their words onto us. How nothing was done
And everything was done. Undone. I had been undone.

And you came years later and now we see each other, you
    and I, crossing paths,
Sensing the truth that connected us, we were meant to
    detect each other,

Reach each other, you and I, weaved to intersect, trust,
  reconnect.
What are you going to do about it, now? Now that you
  feel clearly?
This is you, right in this moment.
Your life in your hands, it has always been you.

I still remember how you went back to your car, you
Could feel it, you were so overwhelmed, you could
Barely hold it in, and you cried so hard, the darkness was
Too much, there was too much of it, and you held the
  wheel
And drove and screamed, your face wet, you burst, across
  the
Highway that wouldn't end, you couldn't contain what had

Been revealed to you, what had lived within you, and you
Felt so alone, with all of it, facing the enormity of silenced
Actions, and you walked through the garden in the
  darkness,
Nothing scared you more, ever, in that moment, but you
Weren't thinking, you walked past his shed, the unused
  shelves,
And you felt the weight of a multi-layered childhood that
  nobody seemed to
Notice, and it followed you around, the dark whispers in
  the night,
You were steered, you knew where to go, you wanted to
  reach the tree,
Yours, that he planted, the one that would never grow, the
  one
That was held back, the one with a network of roots,
  reaching out,
Underground, invisible, the tempests within, electrocuted,
  shoved

Into a corner, and you didn't make it to the tree, fear reached you,

You thought he'd wait for you there, again, unruly, you felt that it
Had been possible, that he had been reached, under the starlight,
Right there, the auburn darkness of the leaves, the sadness of the tree,
You wouldn't meet him, there, not there, sacrosanct, hearing his voice
Again, asking *why you weren't there*, when he asked you to, when *he*
Wanted to see you before his death, lucid, transparent, irreverent, unnatural,
Agonised, tormented, holding on to the skin of innocence,
Wanting to make his peace, wanting you to make your peace
Against your own rhythm.

And I knocked on her door instead.
The door made out of glass.
The room, rebuilt.

(What happened there?)

Why did you go to that room?
Who led you there? You scared yourself.
You scared her. You lost control and gained it.
Then you fell into her arms as you walked out
Of the basement, and you told her that *he* was there,
And she was adamant that he had been dead for years, she knew
What you were talking about and she held you,
You had shared the same monsters.

Häufchen Elend /
Picture Of Misery

A word, out of order, out of your tact,
Could set you off, your mouth, this
Giant net of openhearted darkness widening
In front of my face, the teeth that I couldn't see,
The tongue fallen into oblivion, it had always been

Your voice that reached me, the spit from your screams
On my eyelids, my forehead, I tried to run away, I tried
To look away, but you reached my tipping point, I wouldn't
Let you roam around the house like a madman anymore.

You could wander around the rooms hollering
The worst things, releasing yourself, demonising
Us all, cursing and blaming, screaming that we're pigs,
That we drag you into despair and misery, that we're
Ungrateful, that we don't know real hardships, that we're

Spoiled, that we're disgusting, that *if you die we shouldn't
Dare to show up at your grave and cry*, that we'd land on the
    streets,
Oh, Father, you could paint the worst images in the most
Believable colours and tones and shades, I believed all of it,
Internalised it, let you in, my body, my mind, your
    linguistic
Torture instruments, you never used language to connect
    and love,
You used it to disrupt and tear apart.

You could say all of these things without batting an eye.
For hours and hours. You loathed us all that much. We
Weren't what you imagined. We weren't as easy to fool
And exploit as you had wished when we were born.

I've always had a heart so capable of love. You abused that.
Abused it all. The most beautiful thing about me. Made
    me lose trust.

I abandoned my own heart for a long time. You
    encouraged it.

You got away with saying the worst things to
    impressionable
Children, stuck in a big picture they cannot evaluate, stuck
In the devil's details, thinking the world is ending on your
    terms,
Because of us, because we lived and breathed, because we
    were here,

The evil children that can only take and take, you survived
    because we
Gave and gave and offered and sacrificed and gave
    ourselves up
Because you signalled to us that you needed saving, and
    why wouldn't
We save the one who created us? We didn't know. We let
    our hearts speak.

And you made us weaker. Dependable. It had always been
    a one-way-street.
We ran out of fuel and you left us by the road, kill, hit-
    and-run, we came home,
There was nowhere else to go, we forced our way home,
    and you showered

Us with accusations still, the torment never ended.

And there I was, saying a few carefully worded sentences to you
And you'd lose it.

My chin in your hands, my eardrums bursting,
The volume of your voice as if I existed in a different universe and you
Wanted to make yourself heard.
I had absorbed every single war monologue
That you unleashed with full weaponry in that house, I listened to it, I could
Always hear it even with my head under a pillow, your stuffing voice,

Straight into my brain and memory, of fear, you besieged my body,
I heard it all and took it in, your constant complaints, your fury,
Your incurable hate, and you, the greatest perpetrator of my life, the ticking
Time bomb, couldn't stomach a few sentences of minimal criticism?

The Projectionist

I put myself in your hands, imagining you anew,
Blinded by my own projections, what I wanted to see,
What I wanted you to be.
Misguided, erasing the harmfulness in front
Of me, seduced by the creations of my
Imagination that rendered you bearable,
Desired, and I closed my eyes and you played the part
Because you'd get what you wanted.

I stuffed your body with staged narratives that I
Longed to hear since I had been a little girl,
I had that desire still, and you felt so familiar,
I ignored the red flags. I thought that I was unaffected,
I had no idea to what extent I had been controlled.
I wrote line after line in my head, I wanted to find out who
    I was,
And I'd fit in, in the worst way.

You saw my blindness, my wandering around in my
Own images of you, you absorbed and dedicated yourself
To the illusion of you, my delusion, so you could come out
And play, so you could do what you do.

Empty yourself, leaving traces in bodies,
From one girl's mouth to another, spreading, you, spread, across
Legs, you touched them all, claimed the price, you knew
    that I'd find my way

Back into the trap that I was raised in, and you exhausted
Yourself, falling in love with that forged image of yourself
   that I projected
Onto you to get close to you and myself, to feel alive, to
   feel in charge, whilst you
Put me in a box and discarded the truth that I thought I'd
   found.

Vergissmeinnicht / Forget-me-not

I singled you out
And didn't realise
My father's ways.

You looked at me
The way he would.

I looked at you
The way he would.

Daughters ending up looking like their fathers.

I always knew what my father's eyes had to say.

Daughters ending up acting like their fathers.

I came closer to you. I always knew where Daddy had been.

And I started to taste venom again.

(How many parts of myself did I have left?)

Herzkrampf / Heart Spasm

You erupt at my fingertips, the beat of my heart,
My breath, you burst, your body, the deadbeat skin,
Frowning, all its devastated layers, looking down on me, trying
To swallow me, stomp me back into nothingness, grab
Me by my hair to pull me out, violently, to *make*
Myself worth your while, useful to you, the body of a
Girl, yours to behold, yours to let go, yours to discriminate
Against, a punching bag for your insanity, entangled, I.

Stop breathing, you are too loud, you irritate me,
Go, go, go away, go do something, leave me alone,
What do you want from me, toughen up, you don't
Need this, you don't need that, *I didn't have these*
Things either. I reimagine your scent. I can barely
Remember. I started to refuse to breathe you in.
I breathe you out. I focus on the dirt, the smell of your
Silent decay. Call me heartless. Call me so wounded that
I simply cannot forget, suffocating within memories
Where you burst, your body bursts and swallows mine,
    away, I.

I wish I could write letters of love to you, but
Had I not decided to live, you would have let
Me disappear and dissolve in your cornering presence.

I cut and cut and cut you off, and almost nothing
Remained that I wanted to last, wanted to save.

Selbstkasteiung /
Self-mortification

You thought that you were so strong.
You were convinced. And you were in
Many ways, when you had to fight and
Endure, when you were torn down by
Insults, when they made you suffer, you
Were so strong, but it came at a cost, it
Had always been that way, the slowly
Breaking heart underneath the defensive
Exterior. The terror just kept finding you.

You were looking for something, for friendships
To mean something, go somewhere, for love
To reveal itself, to finally show up, to mean something,
Waiting for the sensation of feeling alive, for your
Path to declutter, eradicate pest weeds, unblocked and free.

You kept falling on your face, one step at a time,
A collapsing house of cards, the endless domino
Effect, thinking that you knew who you were,
You've lived through so many personalities in your
Twenties, I wonder how you could come up for air.

Faces and masks, a blur after another.
Failing to conform, failing to fit in, feeling inadequate, left
    out,
Then too integrated, bored, stagnant, looking for freedom,
Cutting cords, again and again, nothing sat right, nothing

Felt right, they didn't, they would never feel right and you knew
It but you refused to listen to your better judgement, you let
Everything they did slide and slide, and you would always
Drown in your own agitation and helplessness.

I wish I could have been a better friend.
People would ask me about you, and I
Felt so ashamed of you, I blamed you, I shamed you, I repeated
The cycle, I should have stood by you no matter what
Because I knew the big picture, what you had gone through.
I wallowed in my guilt and pointed fingers at you
When you should have been protected and understood.
You did the best you could. You felt what you felt,
Thought what you thought for a reason.
You'd find your way back to yourself in your own time.
It has never been easy. You always fought your own battles and I
Wish I could have had your back instead of punishing you in retrospect
And feeling guilty about all our mistakes when we did the best we could
And simply didn't know better.

Forging Memories

It was your nervousness that gave you
Away, that signalled to me that I should
Disappear, run away from you, telling me
That being close to you, drawn to you, is
Pain-inducing, it means accepting violence as
An independent pulse in my life, your body
Rendering mine fragile, with the permission
Of a child, I, your daughter, where was I supposed
To go when I saw the red flag lighting up in my face?

The nerve-racked body waking up with rage,
Shouting at objects, impatiently, screaming
At its own body parts, damaging its surroundings,
Kicking things, kicking sons, dropping theatrically
On the floor, mimicking the true suffering of sons,
Rendered invisible, the agony, theirs, ceased to matter.

The stampede of your slippers. Up the stairs.
Death seemed near. The visceral screams that
Your voice could produce. At night, you'd lose it.
The smallest of things led to explosions, she'd listen
To your endless monologues, the waste of a lifetime,
The stamina in your sick gut.
I tried to fall asleep with the violence you spewed
Into the walls of our house. You lingered in my body.
You drummed against the night.
Standing in front of a red light. I can feel you losing it.

You never cared about the outside world, about perceptions,
Of you, when people didn't matter, if they mattered to us, you
Laid your demons bare, putting them in danger as well, and for
What, I never got it, your abuse of power, what did you have to prove?
You always thought you owned me, I owed you,
Judging us from your high horse, terror agitates confidently.

You'd lose it everywhere. I took that with me for a long time.
Days turned into tragedies. Nights turned into nightmares.
Obstacles. You killed your own voice. Your own hate ate your
Vocal cords and turned your mouth rotten, it is visible now, I
Can't stand the smell, enough of you, I had enough for a lifetime.

Maybe I will find my way towards forgiveness.
Maybe I will succeed to filter out the particles of love
That weren't destroyed into the failed process of your obliteration of me.
I'm still here.
Maybe I can rid myself of your shadows that you attached
To my heel to survive, to endorse your legacy.
You always thought you did so well.
I always wondered how you could actually believe that.
You forged memories, idealising yourself in the process
And you crushed my truths with your lies.
Maybe I will find the words to forgive you.
But all that anger and sorrow that I could never release

In reaction to yours, first need to be exhaled and unleashed
Before I can even think about forgiveness.
It's my life you toyed with after all.
My
Life
Is
Not
A
Toy.
It takes a lot of steps to reach a greater view.

Beschwörung / Evocation

There's a reason why
You are still coming back
To tell me things.

The strongest resource I have
Is my inner child.

I feel with you
But I stopped suffering with you.

Love
Is all I ever wanted to do.

It would be an unaccomplished story
If I looked back and discovered that
I haven't changed at all.

Healing the past through the present
Means nurturing my own roots back to health.

I've been robbed of expression
And I've dealt with all of your aces
And now life resurfaces in the form of language.

Unausstehlich / Insufferable

I learned about the word *whore*
With my father's finger in my face.
(I know where that finger has been)

I knew that he liked the way I looked
When other women looked like that, other girls, but not me.

I internalized that word then and there
And his finger wouldn't be the last one threatening my face.

I reflected my father's excesses
And he didn't like to see himself.
Exposed. Out of control. Finger on the wound.

You were the first person to call me that
And for a long time it was the worst insult
That someone could use against me
Because you put all the weight, the family history,
The secrecies, the betrayals, into that name,
Your own shame, appetite, self-disgust and fury,
Loaded like a gun, *whore*, your lust and your reprehension,
The conflicting facets in-between, into my teenage face,
And I was haunted.

Everything that word meant, to you,

Infused my body and I accepted it
As a part of myself, against my will.

You encouraged the world to put me in my place.
You created the world so that I could step into your own pain.
And linger, and *hold it*, and freeze, grow stagnant so that people could
Nibble and do what they wanted with me.

You facilitated men's movements towards me,
As a child, how you rendered me inviting, drowning
Me in guilt, in yours, you wouldn't have it, none of it.
You called me names that you earned for yourself.
You wanted me to learn the same lessons, come to the
Same dysfunctional conclusions, disillusionment, frustration,
You misled me, I had never been free, to choose, even when
I thought I was, that was the trick, nature, nurture, nurture, nature.

You wanted me entrapped in the same dead end world with you.
You didn't want to be alone in the crooked
Nest you built and kept going, disheartened, furious and vile,
You pushed my head into your own deadness,
Empowering yourself, decreasing my self-worth with your insults,
You wanted me to become the word,
Become the meaning behind it, the weight, the abomination, the
Sexualised girl with no way out,
But letting you in and all the way through.

Schamlos / Shameless

You learned her language and then
You turned her into a blank page.
Every time you put your hands on
Her skin, grains of sand on blood wounds,
Clenching her jaw, she stopped breathing.
(You didn't like the sound)

Composed herself on the inside,
Meaning crawling into a hole within herself,
To steel her body, to let you do what you always had to do,
And to not die, to survive your touch, your needs and
    desires,
But all she really wanted to do was to bite your face off.
(It didn't matter how young she was, you needed comfort)

You whispered acid into her ears,
And she became bitter trying to
Hold it together, she was bursting,
She mumbled that she wanted to die,
And you kept making it worse, you
Made her think that there was no way out,
That you were it, and you betrayed her,
Betrayed her life, every piece of it,
Infiltrated. How dare you?
(You were taught that women were incessant givers and
    suppliers
And if they didn't give, you'd take)

You'd watch her fall apart right
In front of your eyes, your business,
Card, never on the table, you made her beg,
You enjoyed seeing the pain that you
Inflicted on her face, in her eyes torn apart
By endless tears without words, you thought she
Was weak, but it was you, you who pretended,
You who failed, you who never truly felt anything.

You controlled her, dominated her, you made
Her lose her mind, you felt so powerful, didn't you?
That you could break what had already been broken
And you knew it, you fucking knew it. Reassembling
The shards of her in such a way that you knew they
Would never work, in her favour.

Widerwärtig / Sickening

You always found ways to blame her.
Making her believe that everything
Was her fault.
(*I'll show you how strong you really are*)
You looked at her and
You have been trained to find the child
Within women, within girls, broken ones,
And you'd put your arms around her, talk
To her about love, luring her into your traps,
Tightening the grasp around her throat, around
Her heart, tighter, tighter, grooming her, telling
Her everything that she never heard but always
Longed to hear, needed to hear, you did it, you
Said all these things, but you didn't feel them,
At all, you poisoned her mind and she had been programmed
To think that you were both on the same page.

You abused it. You abused her. You wouldn't let her go.
Your poison spread within her and she kept romanticising
Your tumorous reach, your cock marking its territory, you
Sickened her, more and more fragile she became, and
You rejoiced as you grew stronger, she numbed herself,
Imprisoned, subservient, you spread her legs,
You forced your lust on her without a word,
(She had words for hers you'd never begin to comprehend)
She was yours to take without a question, yours to fuck
    and possess.

You desecrated her, categorised women, it would never be enough.
You were still bursting. You'd fuck other women and fall into bed, where

She slept, where she had stopped waiting, where she fell into despair,
Sleeping, knowing, maybe, you stank, you were drunk, careless, heartless,
Reckless, hungry for women, and you touched her, she was asleep, you never
Cared, gluttonous, you wanted more, still reeking from your escapades,
Sweat, saliva, unwashed, it's not enough, it turned you on to spread the fluids,
Involving her body, without asking, without her knowledge, you thief.

And you still had the rotten guts to blame her, to torture her, to make
Her feel so guilty for all the things that she knew and you did wrong,
You never took responsibility for anything, you pretended to be her friend
But you brought her down, you almost killed her, and still you idealise
Yourself, justifying your actions, or not admitting anything, denying her
Your truths, gaslighting her,
You still seduced her with a word she never heard and so longed to hear,
Your despicable mouth, you disgust me.
She still suffers from the wounds you inflicted,
Killing the love that she found within her
After everything that happened to her.

You know nothing about it, you loathe women, you just demand what you need
And force them on their knees, lies, lies, lies, all around you, pest weeds, you.

Bonhomme

I forgot how to breathe.
In the same room with you
I forgot how to breathe, it was too loud,
Too this, too that, I was so scared, to make a sound,
The wrong one, afraid to upset you, with the presence
Of my voice, by breathing, I learned that I shouldn't be
Heard, that I shouldn't eat, that I should do what men say,
What they desire, not listen to my own body, overwrite it.

I thought that if I pretended to sleep, nothing could
    happen to me.
It made it easier for you. It invited you in even more.
Screaming, the body language, annoyed, repulsed, careless.
You were convinced that I needed to suffer and go through
Everything you went through. You felt superior, looked
At my misery and boasted because you already went
    through it.
You orchestrated and trivialised it.
Nobody would be a greater martyr than you.

You let them get away with it.
You didn't care. You never did.
I swallowed my breaths to accommodate you.
To render myself invisible to not be a target anymore.
You wouldn't stop there.
You'd use your violence against anyone
In any state, nobody mattered. The women you devoured

Like cattle, described like merchandise, holes, holes, holes,
To be filled, to be stuffed and ripped open, trashed,
   ghosted.
I am a girl in the same room with you.
Holding on to the blanket as if it could save me.
Closing my eyes as if you could actually disappear.
Keeping my hands to myself, my thighs tightly shut
As if you wouldn't use your strength against me and
   mislead them,
Open them, by force and manipulation, the voice so soft,
   so suddenly.

Basementgirl | Monsterstory

She smelled his nakedness and shut down.
He held himself confidently and said
Some women are just good for emptying my balls
And for others, if I care, I put some effort in.
*
There was a time when she thought that it was a compliment
When he sent her photographs
Of his cum on his foiled-off laptop screen
Where her face appeared on a picture that her little sister had taken.
*
And you kept it to yourself
When they sent her from one psychologist to another.
*
When she couldn't keep her hands to herself
As a five-year-old,
What were *you* thinking?
*
I need to please.
*
I know how to play.
*
Parents and teachers knock on their door.
*
And you kept your mouth shut.
*

It was easier to handle a child than a household tyrant.
*

And she learned that she could be put to good use.
She told herself that this is who she was to reclaim her autonomy
And grew comfortable in the basements that they'd put her in.

In nōmine Pătris

We remained invisible to you.
Of no importance. A bottomless
Pit of childlike love, subservient to you,
Mercy on you, pitying you (you thrived),
Putting you first, taking in all the pain
That you amassed day after day after day,
Overfeeding us with poison, and we looked
For love with our heads in the abyss.

I observe the undercurrent of death in my dreams,
A body hanging by a thread, obsessed, we disentangled
    ourselves,
The marks on our throats, your rotten hands, the director,
Squeezing my flesh, facial, squeezing, taking my life,
My autonomy, begging for protection, you got me fucked,
    and fucked,
And still you'd accuse me, you'd curse me, send me to dark places
And then blaming me for falling on my face, your actions
In my body would never be your responsibility.

I wonder how many people really knew you.
You set the stage so well, the lighting, you,
In the sedated limelight. You selected people,
You portrayed yourself, you had all your
Personae ready to go, what a feast. You badmouthed us
And they believed that we were the devil himself.
(Scorched earth, nobody ever asked why)

The heartless absent devilchildren, abandoning you,
    leaving you to die
And rot and disintegrate, without mercy, without love.

And they'd never ask why, it would never matter.

I
Am
Disobedient
Now.

They judge us, stuck in their ridiculous ignorance that you
Created and abused. You did this. You made
Sure you were remembered the right way by
The masses of blind sycophants, your life's work,
Your legacy, you rendered the truth incompatible
With the ideal image. They cling to it, suck it, on their
    knees.
Very well. You've established those walls. Fair enough.
All yours. Let them stay in their dream lands.

They would never question anything.
Why we couldn't speak your language.
Why we created a safe distance from you.
Why we struggled in our lives, in our relationships.
Why we let people treat us like trash and misconstrued it
    as love.
Why we let you infect us with your violence.
Why we cried in silence and as loudly as we possibly could
To free ourselves from you and your terrors.
Why we accepted the wrong people around us.
Why we sold ourselves short.
Why we always thought the worst of ourselves.
Why we were convinced that we were worthless, useless, to
    be abused,

Tyrannised, bullied, laughed at, threatened, guilt-tripped,
    neglected.
I was there. I endured. I endured you.
Every piece of you. All that gaslight insanity.
I put it on my shoulders. I was a child.
I'd always remain a child. I'd provide boys
And men with what they needed,
What I was good for, as a girl, isn't that right, Father?

Then I became a piece of flesh, sinful, an abomination,
You didn't teach me well, you didn't show me,
You didn't live it, don't you understand, those fragmented
Disconnected parts of us, looking for you, looking for
    affection,
Were direct reflections of you and your actions and your
Presence and your absence, cries for help, helplessness,
We, you, always, suffering, falling on our faces, no idea
Who we were, studying you, failing you, copying you,
Emptying our hearts out.
And it was never enough, times five.

Acknowledgements

I would like to express my gratitude to my family and friends, especially my partner, *Vlad*, my mother, *Heike*, and our cat, *Cozonac*.

Thank you, *Laura Kincaid*, for being so spectacular to work with.

Thank you, *Maya Beck*, for your unique and magnificent artworks.

About the Author

Laura Gentile is a pentalingual poet and novelist with two degrees in English Literature and Film and Visual Culture. Laura was born in Luxembourg to a German mother and an Italian father and currently lives in Edinburgh.

Laura's intuitive and emotional poetry focuses on sexualised girlhood, narcissistic abuse, the impactfulness of language, psychological and physical violence, grief and the traumatised body, the inner child voice, transgenerational psycho-corporeal memory, raw adolescence and recreative womanhood. Three more poetry anthologies and a German novel will be consecutively released within the next year.